Men-at-Arms • 509

French Foreign Legion

1831–71

Martin Windrow . Illustrated by Gerry & Sam Embleton

Series editor Martin Windrow

OSPREY PUBLISHING
Bloomsbury Publishing Plc

PO Box 883, Oxford, OX1 9PL, UK
1385 Broadway, 5th Floor, New York, NY 10018, USA
Email: info@ospreypublishing.com

OSPREY is a trademark of Osprey Publishing, a division of
Bloomsbury Publishing Plc

Printed and bound by Intellicor Communications, USA

Print ISBN: 978 1 4728 1770 9
PDF ebook ISBN: 978 1 4728 1771 6
ePub ebook ISBN: 978 1 4728 1772 3

Editor: Martin Windrow
Index by Mark Swift
Typeset in Helvetica Neue and ITC New Baskerville
Maps by JB Illustrations
Originated by PDQ Media, Bungay, UK

The Woodland Trust
Osprey Publishing supports the Woodland Trust, the UK's leading woodland
conservation charity.

www.ospreypublishing.com
To find out more about our authors and books visit our website. Here you will
find extracts, author interviews, details of forthcoming events and the option to
sign-up for our newsletter.

Dedication

This book is dedicated with great respect,
and gratitude for his encouragement, to the late

Brigadier Tony Hunter-Choat, OBE (1936–2012)

Commandeur de la Légion d'Honneur, Médaille Militaire, Croix de Valeur *bis*
formerly of 1er Régiment Étranger de Parachutistes; 7th Gurkha Rifles
(Duke of Edinburgh's Own); Royal Artillery; commanding officer 23 SAS; and
President of the Foreign Legion Association of Great Britain.

Acknowledgements

The author wishes to thank M. René Chartrand for his valued help with some
of the sources and illustrations for this book. He also records his gratitude for
the patient advice and assistance, many years ago, of the late AdjChef Charles
Milassin, and to the late M. Raoul Brunon, curator of the Musée de l'Empéri.

Artist's Note

Readers may care to note that the original paintings from which the colour
plates in this book were prepared are available for private sale. All reproduction
copyright whatsoever is retained by the Publishers. All enquiries should be
addressed to:

www.gerryembleton.com

The Publishers regret that they can enter into no correspondence upon this
matter.

FRENCH FOREIGN LEGION 1831–71

FOUNDATION

For his studio portrait in Mexico, c.1866, this légionnaire wears an officer's-style white shirt collar and black satin bow-tie, and a pocket watch on a chain. It is interesting that he chooses to pose with the white campaign 'havelock' cover and neck curtain on his M1858 *képi*; note the latter's rectangular peak with rounded corners, and the chinstrap, which was still not a regulation item. The M1860 *habit* bears the M1852 epaulettes for fusilier companies, in green with red crescents, and the Mexico campaign medal instituted in 1863.

In March 1831 France's King Louis-Philippe, heir to the Orléans branch of the Bourbon dynasty, was just eight months on his throne since the revolution in Paris that had driven his predecessor Charles X into exile. His 'July Monarchy' enjoyed general popularity, but his experience of the fall of three French kings and one emperor in the past 40 years had made him wary. Revolution was contagious, and was stirring nearby in Belgium, Switzerland and Italy. Even the faintest prospect of his regime having to use foreign troops against French mobs was toxic, so he had disbanded seven Swiss and German regiments from Charles X's army.

Louis-Philippe had also inherited a confused military adventure in North Africa, where France had recently landed troops to punish the perceived insolence of the Dey of Algiers. The Dey was the governor of what was still nominally an Ottoman Turkish colony, but was in fact an independent pirate city-state surrounded by anarchically competitive tribes who acknowledged no master. The Paris revolution had left the expeditionary corps with neither a commander nor any clear strategy. It was already suffering significant casualties, mostly from disease, which made the campaign unpopular at home. (In the first three months French deaths in Algiers had reached 400 in battle, but twice that number from sickness.) In September 1830 Louis-Philippe's new commander, Gen Clauzel, was sent out with two equally difficult missions: both to reduce the size of the expeditionary corps by some 70 per cent, and to recommend a future military policy to the new government. The roughly 27,000 French conscripts who would be withdrawn were to be replaced where possible by locally-raised troops.[1] However, this situation also presented an opportunity (perhaps recognized by the Minister of War, the wily old Marshal Soult) to rid the streets of French citiesw of disgruntled foreign ex-soldiers.

A royal ordnance of 10 May 1831 created a 'Foreign Legion', strictly for service outside France. Its companies and battalions were to be composed as far as possible of men speaking the same languages. Enlistment was to be for three to five years, open to men between 18 and 40 years of age.

---

1   Native irregulars would gradually be transformed into regular corps, as follows: (21 March 1831) corps of Zouaves; (17 Nov 1831) 1er & 2e Régts de Chasseurs d'Afrique mixed cavalry; (6 Sept 1833) 1er Régt de Spahis native cavalry; (May 1841) three bns of Tirailleurs Indigènes; (Oct 1855) these absorbed into 1er–3e Régts de Tirailleurs Algériens. Additionally, (4 June 1832) formation, from French convicts, of 1er & 2e Régts d' Infanterie Légère d'Afrique – 'Bats d'Af'.

CHRONOLOGY

Organization and major deployments

1830:
June Gen Bourmont begins landings at Sidi Ferruch, 20 miles west of Algiers, by *c.* 37,000 French troops **(14th)**. Forces of Dey of Algiers defeated on Staouëli plateau **(19th)**.

July French enter Algiers **(5th)**; Dey abdicates **(10th)**. Riots in Paris lead to flight of King Charles X **(27th–29th)**.

August King Louis-Philippe sworn in **(19th)**.

September Gen Clauzel takes command of Corps of Occupation of Africa, to be reduced to *c.* 10,000 men.

1831:
10 March Royal ordnance creates Légion Étrangère, in fusilier battalions organized on the French Line pattern, each with eight companies of 112 men. Depots at Langres, then Bar-le-Duc **(21st)**. Completed 1st Bn (ex-Hohenlohe & Swiss regts), 4th (Spanish) & 5th (Italians & Sardinians), plus HQ and *compagnie hors rang,* concentrated at new Toulon depot, then shipped to Algiers **(late August)**; 2nd & 3rd (also Swiss & Germans), and part 6th (Dutch & Belgians) follow progressively by end of year.

9 November Legion granted regimental flag.

1832:
7 April Transformation of two of the eight fusilier companies in 1st, 2nd, 3rd, 5th & 6th Bns into grenadiers and voltigeurs (flank or 'elite' companies).

1833:
1 May Completion of 6th Bn at Bône.

1834:
25 January 7th (Polish) Bn completes formation, stationed at Bougie.

14 February 4th Bn is disbanded, and personnel returned to Spain; 7th Bn renumbered 4th, moves to Oran.

1835:
29 June Royal decree passing Legion over to service of Spanish monarchy.

17 August Six battalions of 'Old Legion' land at Tarragona.

16 December Decree authorizing formation of 'New Legion' in France.

1836:
26 June Completion of first battalion of new formation; retitled 7th Bn, it is ordered to Spain **(11 August)**. Enlistments continue for New Legion at Pau depot.

11 December New 1st Bn shipped to Algiers.

1837:
18 July Formation of new 2nd Bn authorized.

14 September 2nd Bn completed.

December 1st & 2nd Bns granted elite companies; formation of 3rd Bn authorized.

1838:
8 December 'Old Legion' disbanded at Pamplona.

1839:
16 October Formation of 4th Bn authorized, at Pau; recruits mainly Spanish refugees from Carlist War.

1840:
March Incomplete 4th Bn arrives Algiers **(5th)**; completed locally **(25th)**.

17 June Re-formed Legion granted regimental flag.

28 August Formation of 5th Bn authorized, at Perpignan.

10 October Final elements 5th Bn disembark at Algiers.

30 December Royal ordnance divides Légion Étrangère into 1er & 2e Régiments (hereafter, 1st & 2nd RE), each of three battalions – e.g., I/ 1st RE, II/ 1st RE, etc. Each RE to be 3,000 strong; company strengths, 99 fusiliers and 95 grenadiers or voltigeurs.

1841:
May Separation complete; I/, II/ & III/ 1st RE based around Algiers, 2nd RE (ex-IV & V Bns, plus a third formed from them) around Bône.

1848:
February Abdication of King Louis-Philippe; declaration of Second Republic.

1851:
December Coup instals Louis-Napoleon Bonaparte as president for life.

1852:
December Proclamation of Second Empire under Napoleon III.

1854:
10 May Order transferring 1st and 2nd REs to Army of the East for Crimean War.

June 'War battalions' I/ & II/ 1st RE, with III/ 1st RE to form forward depot, sail for Gallipoli, arriving **21st & 29th**. III/ 2nd RE sails to form depot at Bastia, Corsica; I/ & II/ 2nd RE sail for Gallipoli.

July I/ & II/ 2nd RE arrive Gallipoli; all four battalions form 2nd Bde (Gen Carbuccia) of 5th Div (Gen Levaillant).

August *Bataillon d'elite* formed from grenadier and voltigeur companies of all four battalions.

14 September Elite battalion disembarks in Crimea, joining 1st Div (Gen Canrobert).

October Remainder of force arrive in Crimea; elite companies re-absorbed **(15th)**. Regiments form Brigade Étrangère (Gen Bazaine), 3rd Bde of 5th Div.

1855:
January Reorganization of Army of the East; Foreign Brigade allocated to 3rd Div of I Corps (Gen Pélissier).

Imperial decree (17th) forming entirely Swiss 2e Légion (Brigade) Étrangère in France, to have two infantry regts of two bns each, plus single Tirailleur Bn of ten companies. Existing Crimea formation retitled **1ere Légion Étrangère**.

24 March 4th Bn authorized for each regt in Crimea.

21 June Elite companies among reinforcements from III/ 2nd RE arriving in Crimea from Corsica.

July 400 new reinforcements divided between Crimea regiments.

1856:
16 April Decree retitling Swiss 2e Légion Étrangère as **1er Régiment Étranger**, to be formed at Sathonay near

Lyons, and Crimea brigade as **2e Régiment Étranger**. New Swiss 1st RE to have two battalions, each with six fusilier, one grenadier and one voltigeur companies, plus a chasseur company with men from the incomplete Tirailleur battalion.
6 July Survivors of Crimea brigade disembark at Oran, and Swiss 1st RE embark at Toulon for Algeria.
8 August Units from Crimea disbanded; their Swiss personnel are transferred into 1st RE, remainder into new 2nd RE.
1857:
28 May 1st RE forms *bataillon d'elite* (two grenadier, two voltigeur and two chasseur companies) for Kabylia campaign.

1859:
26 March 2nd RE ordered to form three 'war battalions' for Italian campaign.
April 1st RE transferred to Bastia, Corsica to form recruiting depot **(8th)**. 2nd RE leaves IV Bn as depot at Sidi bel Abbès, and ships I–III Bns to Marseilles **(19th)**.
12 May 2nd RE and 600 men of 1st RE united at Genoa; with 2nd Zouaves they form 2nd Bde (Gen Castagny) in 2nd Div (Gen Espinasse) of II Corps (Gen MacMahon).
June Following battle of Magenta, 1st RE remains in Milan to recruit, while 2nd RE continues with army to battle of Solferino.
7 August 1st RE shipped from Genoa to Corsica.
19 August 2nd RE shipped from Toulon to Mers el Kébir.
14 October Swiss identity of 1st RE abandoned. Both 1st and 2nd RE, each with three battalions of eight companies, henceforth accept all nationalities.
1860:
5–8 February 1st RE shipped from Corsica to Algeria.
1861:
14 December Decree that 2nd RE is to absorb 1st RE, as single three-battalion Régiment Étranger.
1862:
27 February Amalgamation completed.

1863:
19 January RE ordered to form two seven-company 'war battalions' for Mexican campaign; III/RE to remain at Sidi bel Abbès as depot.
28 March I/ & II/RE disembark at Veracruz; allocated to reserve brigade for line-of-communication duties **(1 April)**.
October Formation of 100-strong *compagnie franche*, a volunteer anti-guerrilla element described by Gen Grisot as '*partisans à pieds*'.
1864:
January III/RE shipped to Mexico, plus 350 other men from depot **(1st & 31st)**.
24 February RE transferred to Puebla to join active army.
6 March III/RE joins regiment at Puebla.
1 April Formation of IV/, V/ & VI/RE authorized, around cadres from I–III/RE.
30 April Authorization for V & VI Bns rescinded. **Decree officially restores traditional title of Légion Étrangère (effective 1 July)** for regiment of four battalions, but parallel administrative designation Régiment Étranger is retained.
May Retrospective authorization of infantry *compagnie*

franche (6th Co/ I Bn); formation of anti-guerrilla cavalry squadron, '*partisans montés*' (6th Co/ II Bn).
10 July Organization of four battalions completed; providing detached elements reduces each to five rifle companies.
1 August Final 400 serving reinforcements embark at Oran.
1865:
February Regiment reorganized into three provisional battalions for siege of Oaxaca.
15 April Formation of V/RE in Mexico authorized.
8 July Formation of VI/RE at Blida in Algeria authorized, for shipment to Mexico.
1866:
April Marshal Bazaine receives orders to prepare for repatriation of Expeditionary Corps **(14th)**. VI/RE disembarks at Veracruz **(25th)**. Formation of division ordered **(29th)** with RE as 1st Bde, Austrian and Belgian Legions as 2nd Bde.
4 July Decree ordering formation of VII/ & VIII/RE around cadres from existing units. Franco-Mexican agreement that enlarged Legion brigade will remain in service of Emperor Maximilien for ten years.
August Battalions ordered to converge on Qeretaro.
16 November Six infantry battalions concentrated at Qeretaro. Second cavalry squadron authorized, plus two mountain artillery batteries, engineer company, supply company, and formation of two Mexican *cazadores* units with Legion cadres.
16 December Handover of Legion to Mexico rescinded.
1867:
18–27 February Battalions and detached elements sail from Veracruz for Algeria.
4 April Regiment ordered reduced to four battalions.
1868:
15 February Army order dissolving all elite companies.

1870:
22 August Following outbreak of Franco-Prussian War in July, formation authorized of duration-only volunteer V/RE at Tours, France.
September Formation of a five-battalion 2nd RE authorized, but never actioned.
6 October Formation ordered of two battalions for service in France. German personnel (and Belgians, at their neutral government's request) are transferred into III/ & IV/RE to remain in Algeria. I/ & II/RE disembark at Toulon **(11th)**. Following loss of Orléans **(11th–12th)**, survivors of V/RE and some Line drafts are incorporated with I & II into new *régiment de marche*, allocated to XV Corps, Army of the Loire.
18 December Reduced to single-battalion strength, the survivors form nucleus of re-created three-battalion Régiment Étranger, with drafts from Line regiments and 2,000 new French conscripts.
1871:
7 January Regiment allocated to Army of the East.
26 January Franco-German armistice.
27 March–1 April Regiment joins Army of Versailles; allocated to 1st Bde (Gen Dumont), 3rd Div (Gen Montaudon) of I Corps (Gen Ladmirault).
15 June Regiment sails from Toulon for Mers el Kébir.

CAMPAIGN SERVICE

Pierre Benigni's reconstruction, for the 1931 *Livre d'Or de la Légion Étrangère*, of a Legion fusilier wearing the *grande tenue* of *c.*1832 (the year when the *habit* collar was ordered to be slanted open at the front). The pompon on the shako is shown in the blue of the 1st Bn, with the brass company numeral '1'. In 1833 the inspecting general reported of the German and Swiss 1st–3rd Bns at Algiers that the NCOs were good but the officers too old, and complained – as would virtually every annual inspector thereafter – about the men's heavy drinking.

TENUE - 1831-35.

The 'Old Legion' in Algeria, 1831–35

Formation of the first three battalions soaked up most of the German and Swiss ex-soldiers of the Régt de Hohenlohe and the Garde Royale. A second decree had forbidden the enlistment of Frenchmen, other Swiss, or married men, but these provisions were never strictly enforced. No papers were demanded nor any searching questions asked, and any apparently fit man who presented himself at the depots around the country was accepted. The 4th Bn would be largely Spanish, the 5th mostly Italian and Sardinian, and the 6th Dutch and Belgian.

The 1st, 4th and 5th Bns were shipped from Toulon to Algiers late in August 1831, followed during the autumn by the 2nd and 3rd and the part-formed 6th Bn. They were short of experienced officers and NCOs, and only patchily trained. Consequently, they were inclined to get drunk, beat up their French cadres, desert, or fight amongst themselves (single-nationality companies proved to be a bad mistake – particularly Dutch and Belgians, whose countries had fought over Belgian independence in 1830–31). The first commander, the Swiss Col Stoffel, had to bribe French NCOs to serve, and employed robust methods to achieve a basic level of discipline. By January 1832 the 1st–3rd, 5th, and half of a 7th (Polish) Bn were installed in camps around Algiers, the 4th at Oran and part of the 6th at Bône. The local commanders at first regarded them as good for nothing but to provide a labour corps, for building forts and roads and draining pestilential swamps.

France's first years in Algeria (purely a geographical expression, for a country that did not then exist) were militarily chaotic. There was no accepted power structure among the Arab tribes with which the French could treat. Individual tribes raided outposts in the slowly spreading areas of nominal occupation, and ambushed the supply columns on which they depended. Leaders could be bribed into local peace treaties, but these were short-lived, as the *caids* played the French off against their own rivals in ruthless competition. Far stronger in cavalry, and masters of the terrain, the Arabs could strike static targets and withdraw at will, while French columns were delayed by their necessary wagon trains of supplies. Commanders-in-chief came and went, all of them lacking clear direction from Paris, and there was a rapid turnover of regimental colonels in this thankless posting.

By October 1832 the Legion had recorded 5,538 enlistments, but were paying a high price to malaria, typhus and cholera, while their back-breaking labours were punctuated by a succession of usually small, ugly actions. The Legion's first recorded engagement took place outside Algiers on 27 April 1832, when 300 men took part in a successful raid on a tribal camp near Maison Carrée. However, on 23 May Lt Cham and all but one of his 27 men were wiped out nearby by Arab horsemen, after their own escorting cavalry fled.

The young Emir of Mascara, Abd el Kader, was ambitious to extend his influence, and began to play cat-and-mouse with the French, alternating attacks with negotiations. Operating with other units in mixed columns (typically of a battalion or two, a couple of squadrons and a few cannon), the légionnaires proved solid when under attack by horsemen, and also revealed an aptitude for mounting night raids. For instance, the 4th Bn proved themselves at Sidi Chabal on 11 November 1832 and at Karguenta on 27 May 1833, and the 6th Bn in a raid against tribal villages on 13/14 March 1833. When epidemic disease ravaged the camps, units were cross-posted to maintain local strengths; the Italian 5th Bn took part in the captures of Arzew and Mostaganem in June and July 1833, and several later raids. One to Tazerouna on 2 December was notable for the discipline of the column: during a march of 30 hours, and 13 hours under fire, not one man fell out. In difficult terrain and a punishing climate, the return march of such columns often had to be made in leap-frogging echelons under repeated Arab attacks.

In February 1834 the 4th Bn, much reduced by the expiry of enlistments, was disbanded, and its Spanish personnel were sent home in April. It was replaced at Oran by the Polish 7th Bn, transferred from Bougie and renumbered as the 4th. The Poles had distinguished themselves on a raid up into the Kabylie hills in March, alongside the 67th Line (which was also Polish, composed of French-naturalized emigrés). On 1 July the 1st and 2nd Bns and the central services were based around Algiers, the 3rd at Bougie, the 4th and 5th at Oran, and the 6th at Bône – where the total garrison of 1,500 lost 1,100 men to disease that year.[2]

In June 1835 Gen Trézel, commanding at Oran, led a 2,500-strong column against the elusive Abd el Kader, who reportedly had gathered 10,000 warriors. The three-plus battalions of infantry were commanded by the Legion's LtCol Conrad, and included the 5th Bn and three companies from the 4th. On 26 June the column was ambushed among

---

2 Disease always accounted for the huge majority of French casualties in Algeria. Of 95,665 deaths recorded between 1831 and 1851, 3,336 were due to combat and 92,329 (96 per cent) to disease.

Another drawing by Capt du Val d'Eprémesnil, showing his tent on the plateau of Staouëli outside Algiers.

During 1836/37 the 'Old Legion' in Spain followed in some of the footsteps of Wellington's army in 1813, notably at Sorauren. The location of the action depicted here is unknown, but this naif watercolour shows voltigeurs of the 'French Algerine Legion storming a Carlist entrenchment'. It is by a 'Major C.V.Z.', attached to the staff of the Spanish queen's army in 1837, who described the Legion as 'the best organized [unit] of the army in Navarre... a finer body of men can scarcely be seen'. All are shown wearing coats of dark blueish-grey, and the officer (upper left) makes himself conspicuous by wearing his gold-laced red cap without the black oilskin cover. Note (bottom left) a soldier with a curved *sabre-briquet*, and a white cover on the flap of his *giberne*; see our Plate B3. (Museo Zumalakarregi, Gipuzkoa)

the wooded hills of Muley Ismael, and only got clear at a cost of 52 killed and 180 wounded. On the 28th, retreating towards Arzew, the column reached the salt-marsh of Macta, where their route was flanked on the left by a wooded crest. The Arabs set the dry marshland reeds ablaze, and opened a heavy fire from the woods. On this left flank the 5th Bn counter-attacked uphill without success, and in the meantime other warriors reached the baggage wagons and began butchering the wounded. Conrad, who was on foot and vomiting with fever, rallied all the Legion companies to fight their way out of the defile. The convoy was left to its grisly fate while the troops made a disorderly retreat, led by Gen Trézel and the cavalry. The Arabs harassed them nearly all the way to Arzew, and the guns had to halt several times to fire grapeshot in support of the infantry flank-guards. Total losses at Macta were 62 known dead plus 218 missing, and 300 wounded.

Spain, 1835–38

On 8 July 1835, while still shaken by the disaster at Macta, the Foreign Legion received the news that it had been ceded in its entirety to the service of Queen Isabella II of Spain.[3]

The Carlist War had broken out on the death of King Ferdinand VII in 1833, when the king's brother Don Carlos contested the legal succession of his infant niece Isabella under the regency of her mother, Maria Cristina. In broad terms, the 'Carlists', whose base of support was in the north-east, were traditionalists; the queen's 'Cristinos' were the more liberal party, supported by an alliance with Portugal, France and Britain. Britain allowed a large volunteer 'legion' to serve with the queen's army; the French contribution was the outright gift of the Legion. The Legion's Col Bernelle arrived at Tarragona in Catalonia in August 1835, with 123

---

3 Readers interested in the terms of this extraordinary agreement, as they affected officers and men, will find the details in Grisot & Coulombon, Livre I, Ch 4, and the Appendices of documents – see Select Bibliography.

officers and 4,021 rankers in six battalions. For the next two years they would campaign across a corridor between the Pyrenees and the Ebro, and by winter 1836/37 their conditions of service would become wretched. Both sides tended to shoot any prisoners; the légionnaires were unreliably supplied and often unpaid, and the origins and quality of their officers varied widely, so looting and desertions were inevitable.

Bernelle, given the local rank of general, took the opportunity to abandon the system of segregated units, and dispersed all nationalities throughout his battalions (the method employed by the Legion ever since). From a base at Lérida they were at first dispersed to fight Carlist guerrillas. Subsequently Bernelle took most of them to defend northern Aragon against Carlist thrusts southwards, fighting a number of battalion actions. In January 1836 he was sent to Vitoria to join the queen's Army of the North, and the Legion brigade was integrated into its 4th Division. After costly fighting in harsh weather south of San Sebastiàn, the légionnaires were pulled back in February to man a series of posts in ruined villages around Pamplona.

Prompted by failures of Spanish tactical support, in March 1836 Bernelle (at the expense of his men's back-pay) began forming the first of three integral Polish lancer squadrons, a mountain howitzer company and a

stretcher-bearer company. At this time the Old Legion had some 3,000 in the ranks. On 26 April, at Terapegui, 1,000 men of the 4th and 5th Bns held off about five times their number of Carlists for six hours before successfully disengaging, covered by a counter-attack by the 3rd Battalion.

On 1 August 1836, the 4th Div attacked a strong Carlist force entrenched behind drystone walls on heights above Zubiri. The Legion lancers turned the enemy's left flank and rolled up his skirmish line; the Legion's howitzers bombarded the central defences, and the 1st and 2nd Bns took them with the bayonet while other units hit the flanks. This day-long battle of Inigo cost the Carlists about 1,200 dead, against a total of 200 French casualties. On 10 August, Bernelle announced his departure; his repeated demands for support had irritated both Madrid and Paris. He was replaced at the head of the French mission by Gen Lebeau, and as Legion commander by Col Conrad, who brought out with him a new 7th Bn in reinforcement.

On 14 September 1836, Lebeau sent four Legion battalions into a frontal attack on the village of Aronitz, held by more than a dozen Carlist battalions, while another brigade attacked a flank. Driven back at first by the defenders of the San Gegorio monastery, Conrad's 1st and 7th Bns rallied with the support of the 2nd and 3rd, then drove the enemy right over the high Montejurra ridge and down the far side, at the cost of about 100 casualties. During subsequent manoeuvring around Estella the 6th Bn distinguished itself at Villatuerta on 8 October, before the Legion was reunited in the Pamplona line for the winter. A change of government in Paris had scotched plans to send French regular reinforcements that had been concentrating at Pau, and on 10 October Gen Lebeau resigned; he was replaced by his deputy Gen Comte de Cleonard, seconded by BrigGen Conrad. Winter 1836/37 found the Legion battalions greatly weakened by combat and disease, usually unpaid, raggedly dressed, and shockingly badly fed and supplied; morale was low, and desertions high. In February 1837 Conrad reduced the organization to three battalions.

For the 1837 spring campaign Conrad's 2nd Div in the Navarre Corps of the queen's Army of the North comprised the three Legion battalions plus one formed from their elite companies, two lancer squadrons, and the Legion battery. On 21 March they successfully took and held the mountain village of Larrainzar, but lost six officers, a sergeant-major, and some 50 rankers killed, and about the same numbers wounded in each category. During a subsequent contested retreat on Pamplona the Legion led the way through a snowstorm to the Sorauren gap, and held that village against a Carlist attempt to cut the column. Thereafter it was reduced to two battalions.

Marching south-east to the Aragon front in response to a Carlist thrust towards the Ebro, on 24 May 1837 the 1,200-strong Legion was sent into a fatally mishandled attack on Huesca, where it suffered 350 casualties including 20 officers. Reduced to a single battalion, on 1 June it was effectively destroyed in a savage battle amid olive groves

Anonymous watercolour, formerly in the Brunon Collection, evidently showing a grenadier of the 'New Legion' in 1837–40. The belly-pouch was introduced by Chef de Bn Bedeau of the 1st Bn early in 1837, and the black oilskin cap cover with a squared fold-up flap was ordered discontinued in July 1840. Note the rectangular metal canteen in a dark cloth cover shown slung to the right hip. The collar patches on the grey *capote* are clearly red, as are the grenadier company epaulettes.

outside Barbastro, where Conrad died at the head of his men; Legion casualties were reported as 27 officers and 600 rankers. About 320 wretched and mutinous survivors withdrew to Pamplona, where stragglers later brought their number up to some 500. For 18 months both Spanish and French governments simply left them to rot, until they were officially disbanded on 8 December 1838 and the survivors shipped to France.

The 'New Legion', 1836–41

The reduction of the Algerian garrison by 4,000 men had to be made up, and formation of a '*nouvelle légion*' was authorized on 16 December 1835. The first unit formed was sent to Spain as the 7th Bn, but Cdt Bedeau's new, mainly Dutch 1st Bn arrived in Algiers in December 1836, and saw much hard marching during the next five months. In May, Abd el Kader signed the lucrative Treaty of Tafna, which was supposed to contain his ambitions in western Algeria. Legion recruiting was so brisk (including, remarkably, many veterans of Spain) that the unit could soon put more than 1,200 men in the field, and formation of a 2nd Bn was completed in September 1837.

Attention now turned towards the stubborn Berber highlanders of Kabylia to the east. The following month each battalion contributed companies to a *bataillon de marche* (a temporary task-force unit) which took part in a second attempt on the defiant city of Constantine, perched on a mountain crag. Governor-General Damrémont assembled a force of some 7,000 including a siege train between Bône and

Guelma, the Legion unit forming part of Gen Rulhières' 3rd of four brigades. Marching on 2 October, on the 6th they reached the plateau of Koudiat Aly facing Constantine – the only possible jumping-off point for an assault. Under freezing downpours, Cdt Bedeau's 500 men helped to both dig batteries and trenches and to defend them against fierce Kabylie attacks, until the heavy artillery could open fire on 9 October. Both Damrémont and his chief-of-staff were killed before the final assault went in on 13 October. A hundred légionnaires led by Capt Saint-Arnaud formed part of one of three columns, climbing the breach to fight their way successfully through a maze of barricaded and mined streets against fierce resistance, which cost them 21 casualties before the city fell.

The Legion battalion was left to garrison Constantine; in December the 1st and 2nd Bns were granted elite companies, and a 3rd Bn was authorized, taking strength up to 3,095 men. The dispersed battalions spent 1838 mostly in labouring, but in May 1839 the 1st Bn took part in the capture of Djidjelli. In October a 4th Bn was authorized.

In November 1839, after months of preparation, Abd el Kader broke the Treaty of Tafna and declared holy war. Up to 60,000 warriors rampaged through the western regions, looting and killing peaceful clans and white settlers alike. All the Legion battalions were engaged in May–June 1840 in contested columns between Bougie, Boufarik and Blida, and in the occupation of Médéa and Miliana. Left at Miliana, the besieged 4th Bn suffered greatly from disease while holding off assaults between 15 June and 5 October; the relief force found 208 men on their feet and 80 surviving sick, out of an original strength of 750. The 4th and 5th Bns were again ravaged by fever at Fondouk, losing 216 dead, and 240 evacuated sick when relief arrived on 4 December.

The 1st RE, 1841–54

In December 1840–May 1841 the corps was enlarged and divided into 1er and 2e Régiments de la Légion Étrangère, headquartered at Algiers and Bône respectively, each with three battalions. (According to Grisot

Sketch map of northern Algeria in the 1840s to 1850s. Only the major mountain ranges and massifs are marked as such, but the cultivatable coastal plain only stretched about 70 miles inland from Oran and Algiers before rising into high, treeless, almost waterless plateaux suitable only for ranching. General Bugeaud's campaigns in 1841–47 were based on main garrisons along the coast at (west to east) Oran, Mostaganem, Ténès, Cherchell, Algiers, Philippeville and Bône, with inland bases at Tlemcen, Mascara, Miliana, Médéa, Sétif, Constantine and Guelma. The modern national frontiers of Morocco and Tunisia, shown here for clarity, were not yet established in the 1840s. (Map by JB Illustrations)

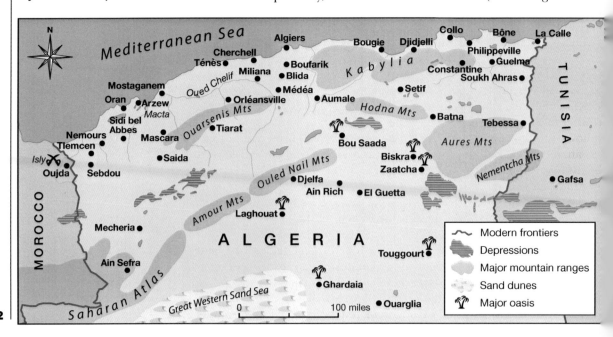

& Coulombon, these titles did not officially change to 1er and 2e Régiments Étrangers until the end of 1856, but for simplicity we abbreviate them as 'REs' from this point on.) The 1st RE was mostly composed of and officered by northern Europeans, while the 2nd had more officers and men from the Mediterranean countries. Both were to contribute to the decisive campaigns launched by the new governor-general, Thomas Bugeaud de la Piconnerie, who arrived in February 1841 with heavy reinforcements, and a clear mandate to crush resistance in northern Algeria once and for all.

A distinguished but ruthless veteran of the Peninsular War, Bugeaud would not wait to react to Arab initiatives, but would take the war to them, tribe by tribe. He reduced his static garrisons to 14 strategic bases (see map), concentrating troops for a relentless series of merciless *razzias* – expeditions of destruction and pillaging. Lightened 'flying columns' carried limited supplies on mules, and otherwise relied upon pre-placed depots and planned rendezvous with slower supply convoys. Columns typically consisted of about 4,000 infantry, 2,000 French cavalry and 1,000 native horse; these would burn villages, kill men, seize animals, take families hostage, and destroy food sources until a tribe agreed to submit. Bugeaud was unapologetic about the high death-toll, but once tribes sued for peace their treatment was fairly humane, to demonstrate the advantages of trade, agriculture and European medicine. Since Gen Bugeaud would remain in post for an unusually long time (1841–47), with sufficient troops for his needs, he was able to pursue his conquest with grim efficiency, and it would be continued by his successor, the Duc d'Aumale.

Resistance was stubborn, but by 1843 Bugeaud had already reduced Abd el Kader's support to the extent that the emir led his remaining followers across the Moroccan frontier. Enjoying the protection of the sultan, he continued to orchestrate resistance from this safe haven, and in 1844 some 30,000 Moroccan warriors advanced to the Algerian border. Bugeaud responded with a forced march by 11,500 troops, and a night attack on the Moroccan camp on the Oued Isly on 13/14 August. This decisive victory forced the sultan to expel Abd el Kader and allow the French rights of 'hot pursuit'.

Bugeaud's expeditions doggedly followed resistant tribes west and south from fertile valleys into hitherto unpenetrated mountains and semi-desert, and the 1st RE's exhausting series of dispersed battalion operations in western Algeria were too numerous to list here. This sort of campaigning involved a constant, gruelling rhythm of marches to keep open the always

Reconstruction of a Legion grenadier, 1841, by the cavalry officer J. F. Eugène Titeux (1838–1904). It shows a blue-grey greatcoat with red epaulettes and collar patches. The cap is as illustrated in our Plate C1, but with a brass regimental numeral below the cockade; Gen Lamoricière's 1843 inspection report on the 1st RE mentioned the addition of unauthorized numerals. The '*cartouchière Bedeau*' is worn on the black belt without a neck strap; the artist shows the bayonet frogged to the right side of the belt, but (as is often the case) has omitted the *sabre-glaive* to which grenadiers were entitled. A natural gourd on a cord serves as a canteen. (Anne S.K. Brown Collection, Providence RI; photo René Chartrand)

'A baggage train carrying the wounded', c. 1840, showing an ambulance wagon and (right) a mule *cacolet* carrying two casualties in seats either side. If wounded had to be evacuated from a column before it returned to base they needed a strong escort; the massacre at Macta in 1835 was not quickly forgotten. (Engraving after and by Charles de Luna)

vulnerable lines of communication, punctuated by raids and punitive attacks by night and day. Légionnaires struggled up high ridges to picket the columns' flanks, fought off attacks on rearguards, protected supply convoys against ambush, established and defended depots (including in 1843 one at Sidi bel Abbès, which would later become the Legion's home), and in any intervals between operations laboured to build roads and dig wells.

During an insurrection led by one Bou Maza that threatened Orléansville in 1845, a notable action took place on 20 September (only days before the famous massacre of three companies of the 8th Chasseurs à Pied at Sidi Brahim). Commandant Mancelon's III/ 1st RE were part of a column ambushed in the narrow pass of Mehab Garboussa, by Arabs who rolled rocks down to block the route and opened a heavy fire down from both sides of the defile. After two hours' fighting the battalion's ammunition was almost exhausted, and they were beginning a desperate bayonet attack up the slopes when relief arrived. It later transpired that Bou Maza himself had been wounded by a shot from SgtMaj Gabrielli.

In April–May 1847, I/ and II/ 1st RE suffered extremes of both heat and cold while forming part of a column led by Gen Cavaignac far south over the high plateaux of Oran province, forcing the submission of Ain Sefra in the Saharan Atlas mountains. In September 1847, Abd el Kader finally surrendered to Gen Lamoricière, and was sent into comfortably subsidized exile; thereafter western Algeria was relatively peaceful, and the 1st RE was dispersed between a number of posts for general duties.

Berber highland tribes were to be found not only in Kabylia and the Aurès but also in the north-west; among the most stubborn were the Beni Snassen, whose hills straddled the porous Moroccan frontier. In May–July 1852 the I/ and II/ 1st RE formed part of Gen Montauban's 4,500-strong column which penetrated their high wooded hills, and for a time discouraged their raiding of peaceful clans.

The 2nd RE, 1841–54

In eastern Algeria the 2nd RE faced the challenge of formidable Berber tribesmen in the natural citadels of the Kabylie and Aurès mountains. The regiment's first task was simply to establish land links from their bases at Djidjelli and Bône to Philippeville, then accessible only by sea. The Kabylies pressed them hard, their pay was late, and initially morale was low, particularly among the debris of the Old Legion from Spain now grouped in the II/ 2nd RE.

In May–July 1842 the I/ 2nd held Djidjelli against repeated attacks, and on 25 August an assault on the II/ 2nd at Bougie came to hand-to-hand. In May 1843 Gen Baraguey d'Hilliers coordinated three columns from Constantine, Guelma and Bône; the latter, including I/ 2nd RE, fought their

Benigni's painting of a Legion grenadier of the 1840s on operations; note the red edging and grenade added to the pouch flap, as described by Cdt Brecht. The donkey carries a portable flour-mill; Bugeaud's flying columns carried ten days' rations, but only had one pack mule per company (and one between every three officers), so they carried grindstones to mill grain taken from the silos of the villages they hit. Looted beasts were killed for meat, but when on forced marches units could not laboriously drive herds or flocks with them, as was the practice with normal columns.

way down to Soukh Ahras to block the enemy's retreat into Tunisia. In June the III/ 2nd at Djidjelli held off two more determined attacks.

In February 1844 all six elite companies formed a battalion under Cdt de Chabrière for the Duc d'Aumale's expedition southwards against a lieutenant of Abd el Kader. The column reached Biskra on 4 March, when at least 2,000 warriors established themselves nearby on the M'Chounech ridge. Under heavy fire the grenadiers and voltigeurs scrambled up between the rocks and eventually took the crest with the bayonet. The column went on to spread destruction through the glens of the Aurès until the end of May. Meanwhile, further north some 760 men of the II/ and III/ 2nd RE were ranging between Guelma and Tebessa (and in the process earning themselves a total of 1,808 francs in prize money from the sale of captured livestock).

The Aurès tribes were still undeterred from threatening Batna and Biskra and ambushing convoys, and annual columns were launched into

Illustration by Maurice Toussaint (1882–1974) of voltigeurs of the 2nd RE at Zaatcha, 1849. Compare with Plate C1, though the cap shown here is the M1840, with a top surface of varnished white leather. The field uniform is the midnight-blue *veste*, and white summer trousers confined by gaiters.

Combat inside a large oasis was at very close range, since all cultivatable ground between the date palms was thickly planted, and divided up by walls and water channels. The mud-brick villages inside the oases were warrens of strong, interconnecting buildings crenellated and loopholed for defence, so when attackers stormed them they needed artillery support and all the skills of street-fighting. (Anne S.K. Brown Collection, Providence RI; photo René Chartrand)

the mountains throughout the 1840s. In 1848 the 2nd RE moved its headquarters down to Batna, where it was weakened that summer by the repatriation, at the request of their governments, of 600 Italian and 600 Polish légionnaires. There is no space here for a repetitive diary of operations; however, in 1849 the 2nd RE fought quite another type of battle, at the oasis of Zaatcha.

Pursuing a hostile tribe south of Biskra, on 16 August 1849 a light column led by Col Carbuccia, and including 600 men from the I/ and III/ 2nd RE, approached a group of oases of which the largest was Zaatcha. Here several *ksar* walled villages – in effect, 'castles' of strong, interconnecting buildings – were scattered amid extensive palm groves, and under the trees densely grown plantations were cut by a maze of irrigation channels and mud-brick walls, all surrounded by a canal and strong perimeter walls. As the column passed Zaatcha it was fired upon, and in the skirmish that followed the French lost five killed and 12 wounded. The column had only

Impression by 'Job' of a camel-mounted French infantryman; while the uniform details are not applicable, the Legion did make this experiment. In March 1853 Cdt Collineau's temporary battalion formed from the 2nd RE's elite companies (minus the grenadiers of III/ 2nd RE) took part in a cavalry-heavy column led by Col Desvaux of the 3rd Chasseurs d'Afrique from Biskra far south to Ouargla oasis in the Sahara. On 18 March, in order to increase the firepower of his advance guard, Desvaux mounted 200 légionnaires on camels to accompany 200 cavalrymen; they covered 20 miles in 4 hours.

one light gun, and some of the buildings proved to have Roman stone foundations. The two assault columns subsequently sent in against a *ksar* were pinned down in the plantations and forced to retreat, with 31 killed and 117 wounded, of which the 2nd RE suffered 14 and 67 respectively. At short range, in close terrain, the soldiers' smoothbore percussion muskets gave little advantage over Arab flintlocks fired from behind walls. Under the blazing sun the column wearily returned to Biskra – which was itself soon threatened by other warriors encouraged by news of this French check, led by a preacher of holy war.

Once that threat had been neutralized, Gen Herbillon led a much stronger column down to Zaatcha, camping on 7 October. He had eight infantry battalions (including Col Carbuccia's I/ and III/ 2nd RE), four squadrons, cannon, howitzers and mortars. An impulsive premature attack cost the Legion 27 casualties, including no fewer than seven officers, before work began on trenches and batteries. The defenders sortied to attack these siegeworks four times between 10 and 15 October. On the 20th, attacks against an apparently practicable breach were driven back with significant casualties. On 25 October an attack across the plantations by 400 infantry, 200 of them from 2nd RE, was also repulsed. On 9 November the arrival of reinforcements brought cholera into the siege camp. The Legion battalions were then tasked with the security of convoys between Zaatcha and Biskra; these were attacked by more than 1,000 Arabs on 16 November and again on the 17th, but fought their way through. Zaatcha was finally taken by storm on 26 November 1849; the Legion's losses had been 85 killed and 175 wounded.

A month later the III/ 2nd RE were high up in the Aurès again, until deep snow drove them back. During the following five years the regiment's battalions would serve in repeated columns all over Constantine province, from Collo on the coast to as far south into the desert as Ouargla.

Crimea, 1854–56

On 10 May 1854 orders arrived for each RE to form two 'war battalions' and a depot for the Army of the East (for details, see Chronology). By 8 July all four units had arrived at Gallipoli; immediately ravaged by cholera, the Legion lost 180 officers and men dead. In August, in accordance with the Franco-British plan to land in Crimea and move on the port of Sevastopol, the Legion formed an advance battalion under Cdt Nayral from the elite companies of both regiments; 800 strong, this landed in Calamita Bay on 14 September to join Gen Canrobert's 1st Division. Marching towards Sevastopol, the Allies met the Russians at the Alma river on 20 September. The French formed the right of the army, crossing the river to face Russian positions on steep cliffs. The Legion battalion followed Gen Bosquet's 1st Zouaves up the heights, and protected Canrobert's right flank in a fierce 2½-hour firefight that cost it 60 casualties.

By 19 October the Legion units were reunited as the 3rd Bde of 5th Div, in siege camps on the Chersonese plateau south of Sevastopol. Placed on the left flank of the second line, the brigade was commanded by Gen Bazaine, a Legion veteran of battles stretching back to Macta and Barbastro. Hard labour in muddy trenches became even more punishing when rain gave way to snow and freezing winds, and on 14 November the camps and stores were wrecked by a violent storm. Although French logistics were not as incompetent as British, their troops still suffered appallingly during the winter, losing 11,458 dead from cold, disease and hunger. There was a steady drain of casualties in trench raids by both sides, punctuated by a few major fights: the I/ 1st RE lost 140 casualties (from a starting strength of 290) during a heavy Russian attack on 5 November coinciding with the battle of Inkerman. Each regiment received about 500 reinforcements in late November, but it was December before the first issues of watchcoats, sheepskins and winter footwear arrived. Légionnaires often crept out by night, both to recover their dead and to strip Russian corpses of their boots.

In January 1855 an army reorganization saw the Legion transferred to the 3rd Div of I Corps (Gen Pélissier). Between January and May the brigade was reinforced with another 1,000 men, but when a 4th Bn for each RE was authorized in late March the battalions had to be reduced to six companies. Capturing and holding a Russian mortar bastion on

Painting from life by Adj d'Escher, showing barracks uniforms of the Swiss 2nd Foreign Legion in France, 1855. The *képis* are red with green bands and piping. The *capotes* (left and right) are blue-grey with red collar patches, and epaulettes in company colours. The *veste* (centre left) is a rich green, as is the sergeant's *tunique* (centre right). The latter has a yellow collar, red cuffs and piping, green cuff flaps, gold-on-red rank stripes, and yellow voltigeur's epaulettes – compare with Plate F1. Note that all wear black waistbelts, the NCO with both bayonet and M1831 sabre frogged on the left side. Another published version of this image shows him with two gold chevrons on his upper sleeve, and without a collar badge.

the night of 1/2 May cost the Legion 171 casualties including Col Viénot, killed at the head of his 1st RE. On 16 May, Gen Pélissier took over from Canrobert as C-in-C; at that date the French had some 120,000 men in Crimea (compared with 32,000 British), and spring saw an increased tempo of fighting on the French left. On the night of 22/23 May a six-battalion attack was attempted on Russian advanced works commanding the extreme left flank. An only partial success was achieved, for losses of 133 to the 1st RE and 209 to the 2nd. The next night the attack was renewed successfully, though at the cost of another 85 légionnaires.

In June–August inclusive the two regiments suffered a total of 237 killed and wounded, but during September the major fighting took place on the right flank; by now the Legion was in the 6th or Reserve Div (Gen Paté). Nevertheless, for the final storming of the Malakoff on 8 September, SgtMaj Valliez with 100 volunteers from the 1st RE headed the assault columns carrying scaling ladders and planks. On the 10th, Bazaine's Foreign Bde entered Sevastopol to garrison the captured city; casualties that month totalled 76.

A foraging expedition in the Baidar valley saw a few patrol clashes, but on 2 March 1856 an artillery *feu de joie* signalled the end of hostilities. The Crimean War had cost the Legion 78 officers and 1,625 rankers dead and wounded. On 17 June the two regiments embarked for Algeria – and a confusing homecoming, of which they had been warned in April.

The Swiss Legion, and Algeria 1857

In January 1855 Napoleon III had announced the formation of an entirely Swiss '2nd Foreign Legion' with an ambitious five-battalion establishment (see Chronology for details). This proved to be over-optimistic, and the depots at Dijon, Bescançon and Auxonne only enlisted 1,150 men in the first year. Consequently, in April 1856 an order reduced the Swiss brigade to a single regiment – but this was to be designated the 1st Foreign, while the former brigade from the Crimea was, insultingly, to become the new 2nd RE. Arriving in Algeria in July, the new green-uniformed 1st RE took in serving Swiss personnel from among the returned Crimea veterans.

The Berber highlanders of Kabylia had taken advantage of the weakness of the Algerian garrison during the Crimean War, and Gen Randon now launched a major campaign of pacification. In April–June 1857, against stubborn resistance, 35,000 men in four converging columns marched across the mountains, including one battalion of the Swiss 1st RE and two of the veteran 2nd RE. (For campaigns the regiments formed *'bataillons de guerre'*, with the six fusilier companies increased to 100 men each and the two elite companies to 120 men. For this 1857 campaign the I/ & II/2nd RE totalled 1,576 men.) The 2nd RE distinguished themselves on 24 June at Ischeriden, where tribesmen holding a steep ridge in strength had driven back two Line regiments. The légionnaires marched up the fire-swept slope and reached the crest in 30 minutes, without firing a shot until they closed with the enemy.

The next year or so saw both regiments performing the usual road-building and small-scale police operations, with the 1st RE based at Sétif and the 2nd at Sidi bel Abbès.

Italy, 1859

Napoleon III's decision to intervene in the northern Italian struggle for independence from Austria, led by the King of Sardinia/Savoy, sparked hostilities in late April 1859. The Legion's weak 1st RE (hoping to recruit Italian patriots) was sent first to Corsica, and three 'war battalions' of the 2nd RE to Genoa, where they were all reunited on 12 May. The 1st RE still had only 600 men, but the 2nd mustered 1,440 all ranks; together with the 2nd Zouaves they formed the 2nd Bde (Gen Castagny) of 2nd Div (Gen Espinasse) of Gen MacMahon's II Corps.

The French marched north, crossed the River Po, then swung east from Vercelli towards Milan. Their army of nearly 50,000 met 58,000 Austrians in the bloody battle of Magenta on 4 June, where MacMahon's corps on the French left won the decisive confrontation. Leading the 2nd RE southwards through the Austrian-held village of Marcallo, Col de Chabrière was killed. It is reported that when he saw Castagny's brigade fighting its way into the streets of Magenta, MacMahon exclaimed

This impression of a similar scene is by the later illustrator A. Beuvry, published in *La Giberne* in 1902. It shows a private and NCO of fusiliers of the retitled Swiss 1st RE in 1857; the uniform is mostly as regulations, though for some reason the top band and quarter-piping of the M1852 shako are shown as yellow rather than red. It has the red pompon of the regiment's 2nd Battalion.

Even in Adj d'Escher's paintings from life the green shade of the uniforms varies, from light to darker. Green dye was notoriously difficult to 'fix', quickly fading with use. (Photo René Chartrand)

LEFT Commandant Brecht's study of a re-enlisted *tirailleur de 1ere classe* of the chasseur companies of the 1st RE, 1856-59, in winter marching order. (Chasseurs à Pied units had included this rank since the 1840s, and the 2nd Legion's intended Tirailleur Bn was to have 30 in each 130-man company.) Since the unit only attracted some 200 recruits in its first year, on 16 April 1856 it was reduced to one chasseur company within each of the 1st RE's two battalions. The uniform is as described in the commentary to our Plate F4, with a brass '1' on the yellow-piped green képi, and blue-grey trousers with yellow seam piping. The re-enlistment chevron on the upper left sleeve is scarlet. One of the background figures wears a red sash with his green veste and white summer trousers.

'Here's the Legion – this affair's in the bag!' This victory cost the Legion 213 killed and wounded; thereafter the Swiss unit remained in Milan to try to attract recruits, while the 2nd RE marched on to the final battle at Solferino on 24 June. There they were held back to protect the artillery, so took only 46 casualties.

After a spectacular victory parade in Milan the 2nd RE were shipped home, landing on 22 August at Mers el Kébir. The 1st RE was sent back to Corsica, but on 14 October an imperial decree brought the failed Swiss experiment to a close. The unit returned to Algeria in February 1860, to be absorbed into a single Régiment Étranger of three battalions, which on 1 January 1862 would record a strength of 2,635 all ranks.

Mexico, 1863–67

Napoleon III's imperial ambitions reached their climax in his attempt in 1862 to instal the Austrian Archduke Maximilien as a client Emperor of Mexico by means of a French army of occupation.[4] He was assured by conservative Mexican conspirators that the people would flock to support a coup against the newly re-elected President Juarez; this proved optimistic, and France was soon drawn into a merciless civil war. By 28 March 1863, when Col Jeanningros' two-battalion Legion marching regiment landed at Veracruz, the French Army's advance on Mexico City had become bogged down by the siege of Puebla.

---

4   For details of this complex episode, see MAA 272, *The Mexican Adventure 1861–67*.

The 2,000 légionnaires did not join them, being dispersed in six posts in the disease-ridden 'hot lands' to guard 56 miles of the supply road from the coast up to the Orizaba plateau.[5] Yellow fever, malaria and cholera immediately took a heavy toll, and by 29 April one month in Mexico had already reduced the 3rd Co, I/RE to 62 men without officers. That day they were ordered to march back from the HQ at Chiquihuite to meet and protect an important convoy bringing gold and siege equipment up from Le Soledad. Three veteran officers of the regimental staff volunteered to lead them: S/Lts Vilain and Maudet, and the one-handed adjutant Capt Danjou.

There is space here for only the briefest account of their action at Camarón (immortalized by a misspelt French report as 'Camerone') on 30 April, which would become celebrated – but only many years later – as the Legion's iconic 'last stand'.[6] Leaving Chiquihuite very early, at about 6am the company had halted to brew coffee when sentries spotted some 800 Juarist cavalry led by Don Francisco de Paula Milan, who was intent on ambushing the convoy. The officers and about 45 men (but not the mules carrying cartridges and water) survived an initial engagement and formed a hollow square, withdrawing through the cactus-scrub until they reached the tumbledown ranchhouse of La Trinidad at Camarón de Tejeda. There they defended an incompletely walled yard about 50 yards across, with lean-to stables, adjoining a two-storey building.

The Juarist force was soon increased to 2,000-plus by the arrival of three infantry battalions; Danjou refused a surrender demand, and before he was killed in mid-morning he made his men swear to fight to the last. The French convoy, hearing the gunfire, retreated safely. In increasing distress from thirst, and pressed ever more closely, the dwindling defenders continued to hold off repeated attacks. By late afternoon the building was ablaze, and only S/Lt Maudet and four men – Cpl Maine, and légionnaires Catteau, Wenzel and Constantin – were still on their feet in a corner of the yard. Each fired his last cartridge, then they charged the enemy with the bayonet; Catteau and Maudet fell, but the Mexican Col Combas was in time to spare the lives of the other three. Of the prisoners taken, about 20 would survive captivity. Two years later and 75 miles away Capt Danjou's wooden left hand was recovered by chance, and would become the Legion's most sacred relic.

OPPOSITE RIGHT Benigni's plate from the *Livre d'Or* depicting a fusilier-company drummer of the Swiss 1st RE in Italy, 1859; each company had two. The képi has a green band and piping and a brass '1', and by this date the greatcoat should have had green collar patches. The drum sling and apron are white leather with brass fittings, and the drum is brass with mid-blue hoops. By regulation he would be armed with the M1831 *sabre-glaive*.

Capt Jean Danjou (1828–63); his position on the regimental staff, as Col Jeanningros' *capitaine adjudant-major*, qualified him for the embroidered gold grenade collar badges. In this portrait photo he is wearing the *petite tenue de l'Armée d'Afrique* (as illustrated in our Plate E2, but here fastened up the front, as in the photo of S/Lt Lenoir on page 33). His triple *képi* lace and sleeve knots would have been in alternating gold/silver/gold. A rather puzzling posthumous painting shows him in a fastened black nine-button coat with the sleeve knots of the *petite tenue*, but the yellow collar and red edge-piping of the M1860 *tunique de grande tenue*; the question is complicated by the fact that in early photos yellow appears as black. (Would-be modellers may care to note that the painting shows the 35-year-old Danjou with mid-brown hair, moustache and *mouche*, and brown eyes, and his articulated wooden left hand enclosed in a white glove.)

S/Lt Danjou had transferred from the 51st Line to the 2nd RE in 1852. He lost his left hand on 1 May 1853 during survey work in Algeria, when a signal gun exploded. He was a veteran of the campaigns in Kabylia, Crimea (where he won the cross of the *Légion d'honneur*) and Italy, before serving briefly in Mexico until his death at Camerone.

Fine portrait of S/Lt Blanc of the voltigeur company of a Legion battalion in Mexico, 1866. Blanc's apparent relative maturity for this most junior commissioned rank reminds us that by law a proportion of commissions had been reserved for ex-rankers ever since the 1790s; at Camerone both S/Lts Vilain and Maudet were officers commissioned from the ranks.

He wears the black M1860 *grande tenue*, with gold bugle-horn company badges embroidered on the yellow collar, which reproduces here as black. Note the large size of the gold epaulette and *contre-epaulette*. The belt is the M1845/58 full dress pattern in gold lace on black, with a gilt plate embossed with an allegorical female figure. The pale line that follows the edge of his tunic is a watch-chain; the red piping can just be made out on his cuff and cuff flap.

After Puebla fell in May 1863, Juarez's troops withdrew from Mexico City into the north. The war dragged on for another four years, mostly in brutal guerrilla and counter-guerrilla fighting. In October 1963 chief command passed to Gen Bazaine, and the Legion was brought up to the plateaux in February 1864. It was enlarged to four battalions in April 1864, to five in April 1865, and to six in April 1866.

Among countless far-ranging columns and smaller actions, one that stands out was a disaster at the end of February 1866 near Parras, where Cdt Brian commanded four companies of the II/RE. Hoping to surprise a Juarist force reported at the hacienda of Santa Isabel, he took 184 officers and men into a dawn attack on the ranchhouse, only to be wiped out by 1,500 Mexicans waiting on surrounding higher ground. One man escaped; at least 100 were killed and 80-odd taken prisoner, of whom none are thought to have survived captivity. The Juarists then attacked Parras, but were held off by Lt Bastidon and his single small company (mainly of invalids) until Cdt Saussier's I/RE arrived to relieve them.

In early 1866 the US pressure for a French withdrawal reached a climax, and the Prussian victory over Austria at Sadowa (Königgratz) that July increased France's need to bring this hopeless adventure to a close. That month the Legion began enlarging to form an all-arms brigade (see Chronology), and in October came the fatal announcement that it would be handed over to the Emperor Maximilien when the French sailed home. Mercifully, this decision was rescinded in December, and on 27 February 1867 the last légionnaires left Veracruz. They left behind them 1,948 dead, most of them victims of disease.

The Franco-Prussian War and the Paris Commune, 1870–71

France declared war on Prussia on 19 July 1870. By early October half the French Army, under Bazaine, was encircled at Metz and soon to surrender; the other half, under MacMahon, had been defeated at Sedan; Napoleon III was a prisoner; Paris was besieged; and a Government of National Defence was scrambling to cobble together new armies.

On 6 October the Legion was ordered to form two war battalions for France. German and Belgian personnel were transferred into the III/ and IV/RE, and just five days later the 1,457-strong I/ and II/RE were already

(continued on page 33)

THE OLD LEGION, 1831–35
1: *Fusilier, 2e Bataillon;* Toulon depot, 1831
2: *Sergent, Grenadiers;* Algeria, 1833–35
3: *Lieutenant, Grenadiers;* Algeria, 1833

A

THE OLD LEGION, 1832–36
1: *Trompette;* campaign dress, Algeria, 1832
2: *Fusilier;* barracks dress, Algeria, 1832
3: *Voltigeur;* Spain, winter 1835/36

B

THE NEW LEGION; ALGERIA, 1840–52
1: *Grenadier,* summer campaign dress, 1840s
2: *Lieutenant* wearing *caban,* 1846
3: *Capitaine adjudant-major, grande tenue,* 1852–55

C

CAMPAIGN DRESS, 1850s
1: *Lieutenant,* Crimea, winter 1854/55
2: *Légionnaire,* Crimea, winter 1855/56
3: *Sergent, Fusiliers, 2e RE;* Kabylia, 1857

D

2e RÉGIMENT ÉTRANGÈRE, ITALY, 1859
1: *Sergent, Grenadiers;* Genoa, May 1859
2: *Sous-lieutenant;* Magenta, June 1859
3: *Caporal, Voltigeurs,* May 1859

E

THE SWISS LEGION, 1855–57
1: Grenadier, 2e Légion Étrangère; grande tenue, Dijon, 1855
2: Fusilier, 1er RE; barracks dress, Sathonay, 1856
3: Lieutenant-colonel, 1er RE; gande tenue, Sidi bel Abbès, 1856
4: Caporal, Chasseurs, 1er RE; campaign dress, Kabylia, 1857

F

RÉGIMENT ÉTRANGER, MEXICO, 1863–67
1: *Caporal, Fusiliers; Veracruz, March 1863*
2: *Fusilier, Camerone, April 1863*
3 & 4: *Légionnaire & Caporal, 6e Cie/2e Bn, 1866*

G

RÉGIMENT DE MARCHE ÉTRANGER, FRANCE, 1870–71
1: *Sergent-major;* Army of the Loire, November 1870

2: *Soldat de 1ere classe, 5e Bn;* Army of the East, January 1871
3: *Capitaine;* Army of Versailles, April–May 1871

H

disembarking at Toulon. They were soon joined by some 450 survivors of a V/RE formed from volunteers in France, which had been mauled during the loss of Orléans. Allocated to XV Corps of the Army of the Loire, the RE took part in France's only outright victory, at Coulmiers on 9 November, but the army's subsequent agonizing winter retreat had reduced it to only about 1,000 men by 10 December. Rebuilt (and greatly diluted) with Line drafts and 2,000 raw Breton conscripts, in January 1871 the new three-battalion marching regiment was sent by train to join Gen Bourbaki's Army of the East for the attempted relief of Belfort. Bourbaki was defeated in the snowbound hills around Héricourt, and much of his army sought internment in Switzerland – though not the Legion. The armistice of late January found the debris of the RE at Besançon on the Doubs river.

On 28 March 1871 radicals in Paris declared a revolutionary Commune, and the new parliamentary government under Adolphe Thiers was forced to withdraw to Versailles. Civil war seemed inevitable, and Thiers and Marshal MacMahon assembled a 120,000-strong Army of Versailles, to face potentially twice that many Parisian National Guards – 'Federals'. The Foreign Regiment arrived on 1 April, but with only 1,003 rank-and-file, of whom perhaps one man in three or four may still have been veterans of Algeria. With the 30th Chasseurs à Pied and the Breton 39th Marching Regt, the RE formed 1st Bde (Gen Dumont), 3rd Div (Gen Montaudon) of I Corps (Gen Ladmirault).

Serious fighting in the suburbs broke out on 3 April, and between 15/16 April and 14 May the small RE battalions were rotated through forward positions in the north-western suburb of Neuilly outside the city

Two junior officers of the Legion pose in Mexico showing differing styles of 'campaign *chic*'.

(Left) S/Lt Farjat, 1866, wears a large straw sombrero; a dark-blue double-breasted, open-lapel *paletot* jacket with flat gold rank rings around the cuffs; a stiff white shirt collar and black bow-tie, a many-buttoned black waistcoat, and a very deep sash, possibly in sky-blue; and *garance*-red trousers tucked into soft leather riding boots reaching above the knee.

S/Lt Lenoir, 1867 (right) wears the *petite tenue de l'Armée d'Afrique*, with white *bouffant* trousers – cut fuller than those shown in Plate E2. Both wear the snake-clasp *ceinturon de petite tenue d'Afrique*, its slings supporting the M1855 subaltern officers' sabre with a gilt three-bar hilt and a steel scabbard.

Benigni's painting from the *Livre d'Or* of a légionnaire of the cavalry squadron formed by the II/RE in Mexico in May 1864. He wears the midnight-blue *veste* with red collar patches and sleeve insignia, open at the neck over the long *cravate* in dark sky-blue; a broad sky-blue sash; and loose *garance* riding overalls buttoning at the hips, with extensive false booting in black leather. The latter, and the sabre and white belts, are Chasseurs d'Afrique issue. For the modified 'hussar-style' uniform and accoutrements adopted in mid-1966, see Plates G3 and G4. (Benigni's inclusion of single red forearm stripes, in addition to the red re-enlistment chevron on the upper left sleeve, is puzzling, since the rank of *soldat de 1ere classe* was not introduced until a year after the Legion left Mexico).

ramparts. At first holding a perimeter around the Rue Peyronnet and Boulevard d'Argenson, they were heavily shelled and sniped, and occasionally assaulted by Federal infantry. One stint of four days in the entrenched and barricaded ruins cost three officers and 15 men killed and 111 wounded. On 20 April, Line conscript reinforcements brought each of the three battalions (I/, II/ and V/RE) up to about 430 all ranks.

The Army of Versailles penetrated the south-western ramparts on 21 May, beginning what became known as 'Bloody Week'. The army drove the Federals through Paris from west, north and south, and converged on the central eastern districts. The RE was brought in through the western Porte Maillot on 25 May, marching clockwise around the inside of the ramparts to join the rest of their division along the East Railway. As part of the northern pincer of the converging forces they fought through the freight yards, canal docks and barricaded streets of the

north-east districts on 26–27 May. Late on the 27th they took a leading part in the capture of the major Federal artillery position on the Buttes-Chaumont. On 28 May, the last day of fighting, they cleared streets in Belleville, and on the 30th they were withdrawn to barracks.

On 15 June they were shipped back to Algeria, where, in the absence of most troops, a rebellion by white settlers had been followed by an Arab rising. In Oran province a company of IV/RE had distinguished themselves in a fight against the bellicose Ouled Sidi Sheikh tribe south of Sebdou on 17 April 1871. Further east, a small battalion drawn from III/RE saw much hard marching in Kabylia in May–June, and between Miliana and Cherchell in August.[7]

April 1871: a shell-battered residential block in the Rue Chezy in the north-western Paris suburb of Neuilly. During the first phase of operations against the Communards the RE was several times rotated from quarters in Courbevoie across the Seine into Neuilly. Eyewitnesses describe fierce fighting in this devastated suburb, with troops entrenched and barricaded in gardens and tottering ruins. On 16–19 April the shellfire and street-fighting cost the V/ and II/RE a reported 129 casualties during four days and nights.

The Rotunda customs house at the south-west end of the Canal de l'Ourcq barge basin, in today's Place de Stalingrad. The building itself was abandoned by the Communards during the night of 26/27 May; the next day the Legion battalions were involved in fighting for barricades blocking the ends of several streets around the junction, before pushing south-east down the Rue Puebla towards the Federal artillery position on the Buttes-Chaumont hill. (Photos by Liebert; Sussex University Special Collections)

7   The history of the Legion is continued in MAA 461, *The French Foreign Legion 1872–1914*.

SELECT BIBLIOGRAPHY

Bernelle, Gen J. & Capt A. De Colleville, *Histoire de l'Ancienne Légion Étrangère, crée en 1831, licenciée en 1838* (E. Marc-Aurel/ Comptoirs des Imprimeurs-Unis, Paris, 1850)

Brunon, Jean & Pierre Benigni, uniform chapter and plates in *Le Livre d'Or de la Légion Étrangère* (1931)

Delpérier, Louis, 'Le Fantassin du Second Empire en campagne (1): Crimée et Italie 1854–59' in *Uniformes* No. 37 (March/April 1977)

Delpérier, Louis, 'Le Fantassin du Second Empire en campagne (2): Le Mexique 1861–1867' in *Uniformes* No. 40 (November/December 1977)

Delpérier, Louis, 'Le Fantassin du Second Empire en campagne (3): La Chute 1867–70' in *Uniformes* No. 43 (May–June 1978)

Delpérier, Louis, 'The French Line Infantryman, 1870' in *Military Illustrated Past & Present* No. 12 (April/May 1988)

Delpérier, Louis, 'The Foreign Légionnaire at Camerone, 1863' in *Military Illustrated Past & Present* No. 22 (December 1989/January 1990)

Depréaux, Albert, *Les Uniformes des Troupes de la Marine et des Troupes Coloniales et Nord-Africaines des origines à nos jours* (Ateliers d'impressions d'art, Paris, 1931)

Grisot, Gen P.A. & Lt Ernest Coulombon, *La Légion Étrangère de 1831 à 1887* (Berger-Levrault, Paris, 1888)

Guyader, Raymond & Louis Delpérier, 'La Casquette d'Afrique' in *Uniformes* No. 55 (May–June 1980)

Guyader, Raymond, 'Le Légionnaire Suisse et son Drap Vert, 1855–1859' in *Uniformes* No. 74 (May–June 1983)

Guyader, Raymond, 'L'Officier de la Légion Verte 1855–1859' in *Uniformes* No. 83 (September–October 1984)

Guyader, Raymond, 'Le Premier Uniforme du Soldat de la Légion Étrangère 1831–1835 (2)' & '(3)' in *Tradition* Nos. 120 & 121 (December 1996 & January 1997)

Guyader, Raymond, *La Légion Étrangère 1831/1945 – Gazette des Uniformes Hors Série No. 6* (Régi-Arm, Paris, 1997)

Guyader, Raymond & Evguenii Ponomarev, *L'Uniforme Légionnaire 1831–1900, 1ere Partie* (Képi Blanc, 2005)

Liebert, A., *Recueil des photographes de la Commune de Paris...* (Huet, Paris, 1871)

Morel, LtCol, *La Légion Étrangère – Receuil de documents concernant l'historique, l'organization et la législation speciale des régiments étrangers* (Librairie Chapelot, Paris,1912)

Rickards, Colin, *The Hand of Captain Danjou* (Crowood Press, 2005)

Thoral, Marie-Cecile, 'French Colonial Counter-Insurgency: General Bugeaud and the Conquest of Algeria, 1840–47' in *British Journal for Military History,* Vol I, No. 2 (February 2015)

Windrow, Martin, *Our Friends Beneath the Sands: The Foreign Legion in France's Colonial Conquests 1870–1935* (Weidenfeld & Nicolson, 2010) – events of 1870–71

(various) 'Homage à la Légion Étrangère' in *Carnet de la Sabretache* (1963)

(online) http://www.soldiers-of-misfortune.com

PLATE COMMENTARIES

UNIFORMS & EQUIPMENT, 1831–71

While all the sources listed in the bibliography are valuable, particularly the extensive researches of M. Louis Delpérier (which draw upon eyewitness watercolours by e.g. Cdt Hecquet, Gen Vanson, Cdt Brecht and Adj d'Escher, as well as documentary sources), the present author and illustrator owe their greatest debt to the published works of '*le Brunon de nos jours*' – M. Raymond Guyader, Conservateur du Musée de l'Uniforme de la Légion Étrangère, at Puyloubier in Provence. Thanks entirely to the works of MM. Guyader and Delpérier, these plates and the accompanying text are able to correct a number of embarrassing errors that appeared many years ago in the present author's *Uniforms of the French Foreign Legion 1831–1981* (Blandford Press, 1981). While incorporating such more recent scholarship, some of the colour subjects are nevertheless presented in conscious homage to the elegant plates by Pierre Benigni (1878–1956), supervised by Jean Brunon, for the 1931 centenary 'Golden Book of the Foreign Legion' commissioned by Gen Rollet.

We have chosen to show a disproportionate number of NCOs and flank-company men, since readers can more easily 'subtract' their distinctions than mentally add them to fusilier privates' uniforms. Regarding dates of introduction of uniform and equipment items, given here in Osprey's house style (e.g. 'M1845'): readers will understand that the official authorization of a particular item always predated its widespread use, since quartermasters always continued to issue existing stocks before new patterns, which sometimes took a considerable time to arrive with units (especially such a remote and neglected corps as the Legion). Also, items given as e.g. 'M1828/32' are those authorized in one year which were later progressively modified rather than being replaced with a completely new model.

A word on colours: throughout these notes we translate both *bleu foncé* and *bleu du roi* as 'midnight-blue' – by this period a true royal-blue was only seen in some officers' items (e.g. the *redingote* of Plate A3). *Garance*, the rich vermillion red of uniform trousers, is untranslated.

A: THE OLD LEGION, 1831–35

A1: *Fusilier, 2e Bataillon*; Toulon depot, 1831

This Swiss former soldier of King Charles X's disbanded Garde Royale wears for *grande tenue* the basic French Line infantry uniform of 1820 as modified in 1822 and 1828, with differences of detail for the Legion (these typically replaced the solid facing colour of Line uniforms with coloured edge-piping only).

The M1825/28 cardboard shako was covered in black cloth with a red upper band. It was furnished with brass chinscales with star terminals, and a brass plate bearing the Gallic cockerel above a star; a tricolour-painted leather cockade, red outermost; and a cloth-covered wooden 'lentil' pompon. This was sky-blue for the depot company, and royal-blue, red, yellow and dark green with brass company numbers for companies of the 1st–4th Bns respectively. 'Lentils' were replaced with red and yellow 'shaving-brush' tufts (*pompons à flamme*) for grenadiers and voltigeurs when these *companies d'elite* were introduced from April 1832.

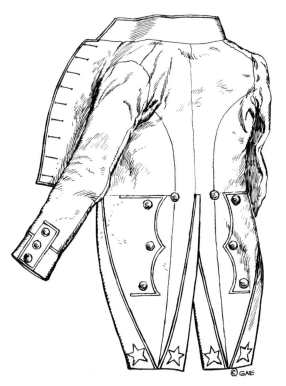

The red piping and turnback badges on the midnight-blue M1828/32 *habit* – see Plate A1. (Drawing by Gerry Embleton)

A T-shaped black 'Turkish satin' buckled stock was worn under the 9-button *habit* coat, which was in a colour termed 'royal-blue' but actually very dark; its brass buttons bore the Legion's name around a central star. The coat was piped with *garance* red (see accompanying drawing), with star turnback ornaments or, for elite companies, a red grenade or bugle-horn. The square, hooked collar was opened to a slanted cutaway shape (*échancré*) from January 1832. Fusiliers wore a pair of *contre-epaulettes*, with padded ends piped garance on both upper and lower edges. The M1829 garance trousers were worn loose over short, 9-button M1820 white spatterdash gaiters (a black cloth pair was also issued), and M1828 hobnailed shoes.

Passing under the *contre-epaulette*, the single whitened crossbelt (at Toulon, reportedly ex-Royal Guard issue) supported both the leather-covered wooden *giberne* cartridge box (steadied by a white strap to a rear coat button, but now lacking straps underneath for a rolled fatigue cap), and the socket bayonet for the M1822 flintlock musket. The new Romanesque M1831 *sabre-glaive* – authorized for sergeants, corporals, and all ranks of elite companies – was slung from a second crossbelt passing under the first. A chained brass pricker for the musket lock was suspended from a buttonhole. The wood-framed cowhide M1828 knapsack was carried by shoulder straps buttoning to toggles on its bottom surface, where three buckles also fastened external flap-straps (from 1832 these were moved under the flap). It had two stowage straps on the top, and a long central strap passing right around the pack. The straps secured an '*étui de coutil*', a cylindrical valise of '*mille raies*' blue-and-white ticking to

The French expeditionary corps in Algeria soon began experimenting with alternative headgear to replace the impractical shako for North African campaigning. These three examples were copied by 'Job' from among seven shown in watercolours made by Cdt Hecquet in Algiers in December 1832. (Top) 5th Line – baggy red crown with yellow tassel, dark blue band. (Centre) 4th Line – red crown, dark blue band and piping; the 67th Line, a Polish unit, wore a similar cap in all dark blue with red piping, but with the crown dramatically slanting down to the right at 45 degrees. (Bottom) Foreign Legion – red crown, dark blue band, dark blue piping, blue- or red-covered button centred on top, brown leather rear flap – see Plate B1. All the peaks have green undersides.

accommodate the rolled greatcoat or *habit*; in January 1832 discs of old greatcoat-cloth were ordered to be placed inside the drawstringed ends, for neatness.

A number of other minor changes were authorized in 1832, but the Legion received old stocks 'without the least order' (Gen Comte d'Alton, December 1833) from depots at Toulon, Auxerre, Pont-Saint-Esprit, Verdun, Bar-le-Duc, Agen, Paris and Lyons. (From 1834, everything would come from Toulon.) Inspection reports make clear that quality, uniformity and fit left a lot to be desired, as did the soldiers' haircuts.

A2: *Sergent, Grenadiers*; campaign dress, Algeria, 1833–35

After the Legion reached Africa the shako was short-lived; Gen Voirol's inspection report of 1834 stated that 'only the *compagnie hors rang* has kept them; the rest have been eaten by rats, and sent back to Toulon'. All French units found them highly unsuitable for Algerian conditions, and adopted a wide variety of locally made '*casquettes d'Afrique*'. That devised by the Legion (see B1) was judged 'one of the best-made and most comfortable', and though its cardboard former was vulnerable to damp it was the model for the cap authorized for all infantry in Algeria on 25 July 1833 (illustrated here, with a non-regulation grenadier's badge), though Legion units initially wore several different variants.

The *habit* was reserved for parades, and the universal field dress was either the greatcoat (*capote*) or the stable-jacket (*veste*), with garance or unbleached white (*écru*) trousers depending upon season. The army greatcoat was iron-grey, initially with a square hooked collar (later slanted open), two rows of six brass buttons, and, for fusiliers, a coat-cloth shoulder strap with the outer end cut three-pointed. A buttonhole in the skirt corners allowed them to be fastened back to rear buttons to free the legs for marching. Sergeants had this superior tailored version (*capote à taille*), cut rounded at the breast, with two converging rows of five buttons, and lacking the rear pocket flaps and half-belt. This example from the Legion Uniform Museum is of a distinctive blue-grey shade, with a cutaway collar bearing patches cut '*en accolade*' in Line infantry red rather than the midnight-blue normally used by the Legion. It displays the red epaulettes of a battalion's grenadier company, and the red-backed gold-lace sleeve stripe of this rank.

Both his company and his rank qualify him for the M1831 'cabbage-cutter' sabre. The knapsack contents included 40–60 rounds of ammunition and dry rations for eight to ten days; the only shelter carried was a big two-man blanket, usually cut in two. From 1834 a flannel body-belt, of various colours, began to be issued for wear under the greatcoat; it was uncomfortably bulky, but an inspecting officer's suggestion that it be replaced with a shorter single-layer type fastened with hooks seems not to have been taken up.

A3: *Lieutenant, Grenadiers*; Algeria, 1833

Officers had a superior version of the midnight-blue *habit* uniform for *grande tenue*, but this second lieutenant wears the alternative *redingote* in a bluer shade, with two converging rows of seven buttons (this was also authorized for sergeants when their men were wearing the *veste*). Officers' distinctions include the gold-lace shako band and gilt brass furniture including peak-edging. Their 'African caps' resembled those of rankers, but varied according to personal or unit preference before regulations of 1840: gold lace replaced the blue piping, and lines of rank lace were often applied around the top of the body. Subalterns wore gold *contre-epaulettes* on the left (sous-lieutenant) or right (lieutenant), balanced by a fringed epaulette; both of these had a lengthways red central stripe at this date. The gilt gorget worn on duty bore a wreathed silver cockerel-and-star, and was attached by gold cords. The M1822 sabre, frogged from an internal belt, emerges under the left pocket flap. (After De Lordey, in Guyader, 1997)

B: THE OLD LEGION, 1832–36

B1: *Trompette*, campaign dress, 1832–35

As infantry the Legion were not supposed to have trumpeters, but they did, for better communication in broken country. This figure is copied directly from Benigni in the *Livre d'Or.* He wears the Legion's original 'African cap' as painted by Cdt Hecquet at Algiers in December 1832; note flip-up leather neck flap, and the large 'duck's-bill' peak (visor). The *habit*, now with a cutaway collar, is decorated with regulation tricolour musician's lace on the collar and cuffs. In his inspection report of 1834 Gen Voirol complained of drum and trumpet corporals adding non-regulation embellishments: red epaulettes, and red elite-company turnback badges. The musicians' weapon was the M1825 flintlock Gendarmerie carbine (*mousqueton*).

B2: *Fusilier, 1er Bataillon*; barracks dress, Algiers, 1832

While the 'African cap' replaced the shako as on-duty headgear, the légionnaire still received a *bonnet de police* in blue trimmed with garance (an inspection report complains that they were 'too low'). The original issue shirt was of linen, with reinforced shoulders and a 70mm neck band, opening 300mm down the front; a circular of 18 March 1834 demanded the replacement of linen with cotton, as already used for the issue drawers. The daily working and summer campaign garment was the 9-button midnight-blue *veste,* with a cutaway collar ordered after January 1832, and from that April with shoulder loops for epaulettes or *contre-epaulettes* (although we show these, they were probably only worn when on duty). Numbers of Swiss and German soldiers from disbanded units retained parts of their former uniforms for barracks dress; this veteran wears the *bleu celeste* trousers of the Régt de Hohenlohe. He is working on the M1829/31 issue garance trousers; partially lined and with a horizontal front flap ('*à grand pont*'), these were worn with braces (suspenders). Socks were not issued, though some men may have worn wrapped foot-cloths. The low, laced, hobnailed shoes were called '*godillots*' after a major manufacturer. For field duty the cartridge box was fitted with a simple white cloth cover tied on with tapes, with the man's serial number marked on the flap.

B3: *Voltigeur*; Spain, winter 1835/36

While they later presented a pitifully ragged spectacle, initially Gen Bernelle was able to supply his légionnaires from stores taken with them to Spain (although we follow convention here in showing local knitted stockings and espadrilles replacing worn-out shoes). The M1833 'African cap' had a black oilcloth bad-weather cover with a neck flap. The greatcoat had midnight-blue collar patches, but the square collar was usually unfastened and folded and buttoned down. The painting of voltigeurs by 'Major C.V.Z.' (see page 9) interestingly shows an old *sabre-briquet* instead of the regulation M1831 'cabbage-cutter', a white-covered *giberne,* and a local water-flask. White canvas haversacks and knapsacks were common on both sides in the First Carlist War.

It is impossible to reconstruct with any confidence the lancer squadrons raised in Spain; they were uniformed using cloth from the Legion's local stores, and were apparently (at least initially) very smart: the memoirist Gottlieb von Rosen called them 'a toy for the vain Bernelle and his lady'. Grisot mentions a cap badge of crossed yellow flags with the squadron number between, strapped riding boots reaching

See Plate A2: the *casquette d'Afrique* of 'conical' shape was officially authorized for troops in Africa on 25 July 1833, though different models already in service could be retained without modification. The M1833 was of cloth-covered cardboard, with a 140mm-high red crown, a 50mm dark blue band, and less dark blue piping around the edge of the pleated, buttoned crown, the top edge of the band, and up the four 'quarters'. Note the chinstrap, and the 'duck's-bill' shape of the peak.

above the knee, a lance with a red-and-yellow pennon, a Spanish sabre and a pistol.

C: THE NEW LEGION; ALGERIA, 1840–52

C1: *Grenadier*, summer campaign dress, mid-1840s

Elite companies of different battalions were sometimes grouped for offensive operations; e.g., on two occasions in summer 1846 the grenadiers and voltigeurs of II/ and III/ 1st RE formed a *bataillon de marche* as part of flying columns, as had those of the whole 2nd RE in April 1842. The M1842 *casquette* had this loop, button and cockade; an unsatisfactory leather-stiffened M1840 version had the same, and also a varnished white leather crown-top. Examples often show the peak clipped to a 'rectangular' shape with round corners, and this became general in the late 1840s. During that decade inspecting generals reported that the Legion wore a variety of headgear: 'the 2e RE still has Old Legion caps, which are horrible' (1841); 'cockades, loops and numerals have been added to old caps which they should not have', and 'it would be better to have a cap without cardboard' (1843); 'many leather caps with white tops [M1840] are still in regular use. Rain and sun have reduced them to unserviceability' (1845). The orders of 28 July 1840 had discontinued the black oilskin cover, but authorized neck-curtains of that material for winter and of cotton for summer. Finally, on 7 January 1850 the *casquette* was officially discontinued for the Legion and the Bats d'Af in favour of a '*bonnet de police à visière*' or '*képy*' (see figure D2).

The New Legion did not have *habits* (Gen Rullière's report, 1837), and the far-reaching Army regulations of 25 April 1845, which introduced a skirted tunic and waistbelt equipment in place of the coatee and crossbelts (see figure D3), hardly

The red piping on the French infantry's midnight-blue skirted *tunique* introduced by regulations of 25 April 1845; the pattern on the rear skirts was termed 'à la Soubise', and the piped belt-loop appeared on the left side only. Regulations of 1 January 1858 would reduce the skirt length from 550mm to 435mm. This tunic was worn in the Legion only by NCOs (see Plate D3); the drawing shows the gold-on-red sleeve stripe of a sergeant, and the yellow epaulettes and bugle-horn collar badges of a voltigeur company. (Drawing by Gerry Embleton)

affected the légionnaire's appearance. Only NCOs wore the new tunic; the *capote* was still the winter field dress for all rankers, and the *veste* the summer field dress for corporals and soldiers, often with the chest unbuttoned and the cuffs turned back. At some time after their reintroduction in November 1837 the elite companies adopted midnight-blue cloth cut-out badges on scarlet collar patches, and after 1841 the two regiments had numbered buttons. For troops in Algeria a dark sky-blue calico *cravate*, already tolerated in place of the stock or a black cravat, was officially authorized in September 1846. From 1841 the garance and white trousers both lost their front flap. The M1832 shoes had a noticeably square toe.

The Legion had anyway long anticipated the updated equipment, by the replacement of the crossbelt *giberne* with a broad belly-pouch at the waist, almost certainly inspired by Spanish examples. Shortly after the New Legion reached Algiers in December 1836 Chef de Bn Bedeau of the 1st Bn ordered his unit to make these *cartouchières* from scrap leather and cloth, and to fit them with a supporting neck strap and a waistbelt, to which the bayonet was to be frogged. (Commandant Brecht describes cloth flap-covers on leather pouches, decorated by elite companies with red edging and badges.) This practical pouch, which lasted in the Legion into the 1860s, was soon copied by other infantry in Algeria, and a War Ministry order of 16 July 1840 called for 30,000 sets to be made up using old crossbelts and *gibernes*.

Troops in the field seem usually to have left the sabre in barracks, and often, for Gen Bugeaud's 'flying columns', the knapsack too. The necessary minimum of clothing, rations and ammunition were carried in a horseshoe roll using the large linen *sac à campement*. The 1-litre M1828 *tonnelet* canteen (made from old oak barrel-staves, and painted olive-green) was still in use, alongside rectangular metal types and traditional gourds. By December 1842 both regiments were fully equipped with the smoothbore M1822 T *bis* percussion musket.

C2: *Lieutenant*, 1846

This is mostly based on a naif portrait by Capt Maréchal of Lt Saal, painted in December 1846 (see page 15). Already at this date his *casquette* is shown as low and unstiffened like the 1850 '*képy*'; we reconstruct it with the two lace *soutaches* and single 'quarter-piping' for a lieutenant. (An order of 28 July 1840 gave officers a regulated sequence of one to five lines of 3mm metallic rank lace butting down against the cap band.) The Saal portrait also seems to show, if indistinctly, a lace at the top edge; no regulation gilt regimental number can be seen (conceivably, because of Saal's secondment to the *bureau Arabe*?). He wears the M1845 *caban*, an officers' hooded cold-weather coat loosely cut for wear over the uniform tunic complete with epaulettes; this replaced the officers' *capote* and *redingote*. Privately purchased and therefore varying in details, *cabans* were trimmed with black silk ribbon, lavishly ornamented with black embroidery including flamboyant knots up the sleeves, and fastened with cords and toggles. An example in the Legion Uniform Museum has the popular bright scarlet lining, but the Saal portrait shows very dark sky-blue. It characteristically shows the coat worn open below the neck, revealing a high-cut waistcoat with many small gilt buttons, and a broad sash of patterned Algerian material.

C3: *Capitaine adjudant-major*, regimental staff; *grande tenue*, 1852–55

Full dress was basically unchanged since the regulations of 4 March 1845, but details of the officer's *képi* were specified on 29 April 1852. It was to be 100mm high at the front, 150mm at the rear, with a 30mm band and a crown diameter of 120mm, a gold-lace false chinstrap, and a round-cornered peak 40mm front-to-back in the centre. In fact, fashionable officers would order it with an increasingly forward-tilting crown and a shallower band, and, as with their tunics, black was substituted for the specified 'royal-blue'. The 3mm bullion lace was single around the sunken crown-top and in its central quatrefoil knot (the latter, double for field-grade officers from 1858). Otherwise it was specified as follows (H = horizontal above edge of band, V = vertical 'quarter-piping'):

The M1845 infantry shako was of leather covered with midnight-blue cloth, 170mm high at the front and 200mm at the back. It had a 25mm black leather band at the bottom, a 20mm *garance*-red top band, and 3mm vertical *garance* quarter-piping up the back and sides. The rounded peak was slightly downturned, and measured 60mm from front to back at the centre. Elite companies had red or yellow double pompons, fusilier companies eliptical pompons in blue, red or yellow for 1st–3rd Bns respectively, bearing brass company numerals. Below a 58mm-diameter *tricoleur*-painted cockade (blue in the centre) the crowned brass plate was edged with laurel and oak branches supported by scrolls, and pierced in the centre with the regimental numeral surrounded by embossed lettering 'LÉGION/ ÉTRANGÈRE'.

We show this headgear because légionnaires are certainly illustrated wearing it by 19th-century artists such as 'Janet-Lange' (Ange-Louis Janet, 1811–72) and Titeux, who evidently worked from the army dress regulations. It is perhaps possible that it was indeed issued to rear-depot personnel at Toulon; however, there is no evidence that this shako or its later replacements were ever worn in North Africa by the Legion or the African Light Infantry ('Bats d'Af'), who were specifically authorized to wear caps instead. (Detail from print by 'Janet-Lange', ex-Depréaux, private collection; shako courtesy Joe Musso Collection; photos René Chartrand)

Colonel, V x3 gold, H x5 gold; *lieutenant-colonel*, V gold/silver/gold, H g/s/g/s/g; *major*, V x3 g, H from top g/g/g/s.
Chef de bataillon, V x3 g, H x4 g.
Capitaine adjudant-major: V x2 g, H g/s/g; *capitaine*, V x2 g, H x3 g.
Lieutenant: V x1 g, H x2 g; *sous-lieutenant*: V & H, x1 g.
Adjudant sous-officier: V & H, x1 silver.

The nine-button M1845 royal-blue tunic had a cutaway collar, which bore a gold-embroidered grenade for regimental staff and grenadiers and a gold bugle-horn for voltigeurs. The 1855 and 1858 pattern tunics would be specified as black, with a closed yellow collar with visible black edging; this was ordered *échancré* from 30 March 1860. Otherwise all these patterns were piped *garance* as here (for rear, see Plate F3),

including a belt-loop on the left side (which was impractical, and was in fact never worn over the belt).

Bullion *brides* secured the epaulettes. These were flat, with one thick between two thinner crescents, 80mm-long narrow twist fringes for company officers (including *capitaine adjudant-major*) and 60mm thicker fringes for field grades. They were worn as follows (all gold unless specified silver): *colonel*, two; *lieutenant-colonel*, two, straps silver, crescents and fringes gold; *major & chef de bataillon*, epaulette on right, contre-epaulette on left; *capitaine adjudant-major*, two silver; *capitaine*, two; *lieutenant*, epaulette left, contre-epaulette right; *sous-lieutenant*, epaulette right, contre-epaulette left.

The gorget now has a silver applied eagle-and-thunderbolt motif, with an added crown after 1852. The trousers are strapped beneath the shoes. The gold-laced M1845 *ceinturon*

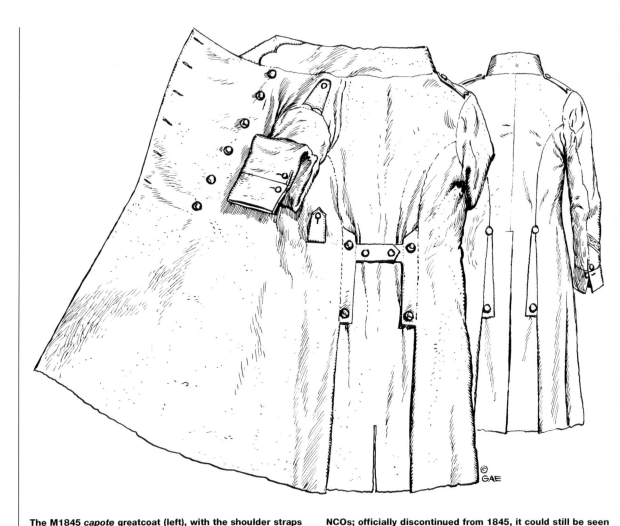

The M1845 *capote* greatcoat (left), with the shoulder straps for fusilier companies; these were replaced with loops to retain epaulettes from March 1852. The vertical rear flaps covered internal pockets, and the skirt corners were usually carried back to the lower button. The buttoning belt-loop on the left side was lined with leather. The lateral space between the two rows of six front buttons was originally tapered from 240mm at the top to 140mm at the bottom. The brass buttons were 23mm and 17mm in diameter.
(Right) Rear of the superior *capote à taille* authorized for

NCOs; officially discontinued from 1845, it could still be seen in the 1850s (see Plates A2 and E1).
Changes to the greatcoat were minor. The M1858 had the collar lowered from 60mm to 55mm, and the M1867 to 45mm with rounded front corners; the latter had the button pairs spaced 160mm apart at the top tapering down to 140mm. Neither the M1855 nor M1860 coats, with turn-down collars and other detail differences, were issued to the Legion. (Drawing by Gerry Embleton)

de grande tenue supports the M1845 subaltern's sabre. Company officers wore white cotton gloves, field officers white kid leather.

D: CAMPAIGN DRESS, 1850s
D1: *Lieutenant, Brigade Étrangère*; Crimea, winter 1854/55
Copied from an anonymous watercolour, this is a typical example of officers' individuality in campaign dress. His officer's *képi* is the M1852. Over his M1845 tunic he wears a privately acquired naval *caban* with both a hood and a cape, his rank being marked by two flat gold-braid rings around the cuffs. His trousers are tucked into private-purchase boots. The visible display of coloured flannel body-belts, long worn

under field clothing, was now becoming tolerated and fashionable. His M1845 sabre scabbard is suspended from the popular *ceinturon de petite tenue d'Afrique*, with a gilt snake-and-discs clasp.

D2: *Légionnaire, Brigade Étrangère*; Crimea, winter 1855/56
Regulations of 17 January 1850 had replaced the *casquette d'Afrique* for the Legion and Africa Light Infantry with this '*bonnet de police à visière*' in the same colours, with a large rectangular peak with rounded corners. Two years later its use was extended to Line troops sent to North Africa, hence it is usually termed the 'M1852 *képi*'. For rankers it measured 140mm high at the front and 160mm at the rear; it would here

display the regimental number of the 1st RE in red, and is tied on against the wind with a locally acquired cloth.

In winter 1854/55 the government failed to provide tents, but did supply the troops freezing in the trenches before Sevastopol with 60,000 'Criméenne' watchcoats of differing materials and patterns; some had capes, some hoods, and some both, and side pockets with or without horizontal flaps. General Vanson described coats of midnight-blue for the Line and blue-grey for the Light Infantry, and British Army grey caped greatcoats were also acquired. In 1855/56 three types were issued: in blue-grey greatcoat cloth or midnight-blue, with two rows of brass half-ball buttons; and hooded but capeless coats in light reddish-brown with one row of black bone or wood buttons. The men's use of body-belts outside the coat (of red, sky-blue and other shades, randomly) was now tolerated (when tightly wound they gave good back support), as were *musette* haversacks whose details probably varied. Instead of a single-spout metal canteen (see E1), Benigni shows a leather flask. Locally made knee-length gaiters in brown or grey canvas were wrapped or stuffed with straw, and our man wears sheepskin foot-cloths with Russian wooden clogs, though *sabots* were also shipped out from France. He has made himself mittens from the skin of a dog (which doubtless ended up in the cooking pot).

D3: Sergent, Fusiliers, 2e Régiment Étranger; Kabylia, 1857

Back in Africa, this Crimea veteran of either II/ or III/ 2nd RE is serving in 1st Bde (Gen Bourbaki) of 2nd Div (Gen MacMahon) during Gen Randon's major offensive against the Kabylie Berber tribes. He exemplifies the dress of NCOs when corporals and privates were wearing the *veste*; in contrast to the Swiss 1er RE (Plate F), they were the only légionnaires of the 2e RE to wear the 1845-pattern *tunique* in the field. Of midnight-blue, it was piped garance (see line drawing on page 40). By an order of 30 March 1852 the contre-epaulettes of fusilier companies were replaced with fringed green epaulettes with red crescents. (The former had not been worn on *capotes,* but the latter were; greatcoats therefore had their old three-pointed shoulder straps of coat cloth replaced with loops.) The tunic is worn with the M1852 *képi;* the sky-blue calico cravat; garance trousers; and M1855 gaiters over M1832 shoes.

The only visible part of his belt kit is the big M1845 *giberne* at centre rear, but his bayonet and sabre scabbards are frogged to his left hip. (This campaign saw the first issue of a new conical Nessler bullet, with an expanding lead skirt around a hollow base, to improve the performance of the smoothbore musket; maximum range increased to 400 yards.) The 66cm-long M1831 *sabre-glaive* was still regulation for NCOs, corporals, pioneers, musicians, and all ranks of the elite companies, but if carried at all it was mostly used as a camping tool.

Since 1848 the straps of the M1845/48 knapsack had been black, and the carrying-straps had become 'upside-down Ys' buttoned in front of the shoulders to *contre-sanglons* passing down in front to hook to belt slides, thus supporting the weight of the belt kit. Various campaign tents had been tried (e.g. in 1839, 16-man tents), but transporting them for troops 'on column' took up too much space in baggage wagons. In the 1840s men had to improvise by cutting their big two-man blankets and their *sacs à campement* and using

This unfinished watercolour sketch of a soldier of the 1st RE in Crimea, 1855, is still worth studying, since it is supposedly by Gen Joseph Émile Vanson (1825–1900), perhaps the leading eyewitness artist of the armies of the Second Empire. While much is obscure, note the midnight-blue collar patches on the M1845/52 greatcoat, and the large size of the frontal belt pouch from which the légionnaires got their nickname of *ventres de cuir* – 'leather-bellies'. (ex-Depréaux, private collection; photo René Chartrand)

muskets or branches to rig up minimal shelters, but since February 1855 a man-portable bivouac tent had finally been issued, with a single 1.2m pole. Spare clothing is folded under the tent/blanket roll, and the M1852 individual mess tin (*gamelle*) is strapped on top.

E: 2e RÉGIMENT ÉTRANGER, ITALY, 1859

E1: Sergent, Grenadiers; Genoa, May 1859

The M1858 *képi* was reduced in height to 120mm at the front, 140mm at the rear, and non-regulation brass regimental numbers were now tolerated. Some illustrations show chinstraps. The Legion never received the M1855 *capote* with

Benigni's splendidly characterful impression of a veteran légionnaire of the Second Empire on column in Algeria in the late 1850s. He has the collar and cuffs of his *capote* opened and folded back, as usual when marching at ease. The M1845/48 knapsack is stowed with the M1855 tent-roll and its single pole nearly 4 feet long – see Plate D3.

turn-down collar; the M1845/58 had a 55mm cutaway collar bearing *pattes en accolade* in midnight-blue instead of the Line's red. Although officially discontinued since 1845 this NCO-pattern tailored variant, of superior cut in a bluer shade, was still to be seen, with its two converging rows of five buttons. Note here the grenadier-company epaulettes, and the red-backed gold sleeve stripes of rank. The proudly displayed decorations are the Medaille Militaire for gallantry, and the British Crimea Medal with 'Alma' clasp awarded to men of the elite battalion that fought there. Flank-company men were supposed to wear a moustache and a 'mouche' lip tuft, but fusiliers moustaches only.

The Legion's big leather belly-pouch dominates his belt kit, and he does not seem to carry the M1831 *glaive*. Canteens were not Army regulation items, being issued by units as part of the campaign equipment; the common metal 1-litre, single-spout type was rectangular, about 16cm x 14cm and covered with old greatcoat cloth. Note that he does not yet have a regulation *musette* or a mug. His backpack is the new

M1854 *havresac* (see E3); the front *contre-sanglons* of the 1848 Y-shaped strap arrangement mean that the 'Bedeau' pouch no longer needs its own support strap around the neck. Officially four reserve packets of cartridges were still carried rather inaccessibly in the knapsack, so in Italy the 'leather-bellies' from Africa were more conveniently equipped than the *lignards*. The M1842 T percussion musket was rifled from 1857 onwards, earlier weapons being called in progressively for modification.

E2: *Sous-lieutenant*; Magenta, June 1859

This classic Second Empire infantry subaltern of l'Armée d'Afrique, fashionably dressed in the face of battle, is a composite based on portrait photos. Over a white shirt with a black satin bow-tie he wears a high-cut black waistcoat with many small gilt buttons, and a very broad sash which might be either sky-blue or red. The black coat is the extremely popular 9-button '*petite tenue de l'Armée d'Afrique*', a straight frock coat very often worn opened below the shallow, rounded, standing collar. In the lower sleeves long rear vents reveal red lining behind many tiny gold thread loops engaging ball buttons on the rear edge. Rank was indicated by extensive gold sleeve knots; sous-lieutenants wore these as a continuation of their single flat gold cuff braid, and more senior ranks in multiples of 3mm gold lace to match the *képi*. The fashionable cuts for trousers were a very *bouffant* Turkish style, or this '*mi-bouffant*' like the Chasseurs à Pied; at Magenta all ranks wore white summer trousers. The outfit is finally set off by the *caban* (see C2), rolled and slung with its scarlet lining outwards. Over his sash he wears the 'African undress belt' with its snake-and-discs clasp, supporting an M1855 subaltern's sabre with its all-steel scabbard.

E3: *Caporal, Voltigeurs*, May 1859

He carries the *marmite de campement* ('*bouthéon*'), of which one was issued to each squad along with a larger, similarly shaped water can (*grand bidon*) with a different lid, and a flat cooking dish (*grande gamelle*); all these were carried strapped to the outside of the pack. By this date a new canteen with two spouts was available, but the *musette* tolerated in Crimea seems not to have been generally used in Italy. The M1858 greatcoat, with its skirts buttoned back to the rear pocket flaps, is 'blued-iron grey'. As in figure E1, here it shows elite-company epaulettes and forearm rank stripes – and again, the M1831 *glaive* to which he is entitled is not carried. The M1855 gaiters had 11 buttonholes but six extra upper buttons set further back, to allow adjustment for fit. The new M1854 *havresac* had upper and lower stowage straps each side to secure the tent-roll containing the blanket (and when necessary, the greatcoat); the tent now came with a two-section pole, wooden pegs and cords. Beneath the roll are stowed the garance trousers and midnight-blue *veste*; on top are attached the *gamelle individuelle*, and the firewood that soldiers always gathered whenever opportunity offered.

F: THE SWISS LEGION, 1855–59

F1: *Grenadier, 2e Légion Étrangère*; Dijon, 1855

This early recruit prepares to go on parade at the first depot, wearing the tunic that in this formation was issued to all non-commissioned ranks. The regulations of 30 January and 22 February 1855 gave the Swiss the Line's 1845/55 pattern but in green, with garance cuffs and piping, and a closed yellow collar piped green and bearing red badges for elite companies. The tunic colour was officially *verte claire*, but some paintings

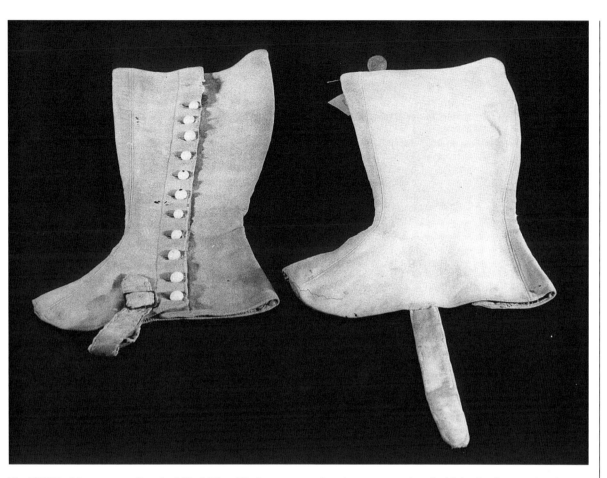

The M1855 white canvas gaiters had 11 visible white bone buttons, but the upper six were duplicated sideways in a second row, for size adjustment – see Plate E3. The cloth under-straps were replaced with leather by an order of October 1865; in 1867 the number of buttons was reduced to nine, with the upper five duplicated.

by Adj Escher show this richer shade. Fusiliers wore M1852 epaulettes in green with red crescents, and voltigeurs all-yellow. Note a re-enlistment chevron on the left sleeve; some Swiss personnel were veterans who were transferred in from existing units. The M1852 shako had a sunken leather top, a rigid black cloth body with ventilators, a garance top band and quarter-piping, and a black leather band and peak. It was furnished with a brass eagle plate, and (from 1856) with chinscales. Elite companies had double pompons, and fusiliers oval pompons in battalion colours (blue, red and yellow respectively) which might bear the brass regimental number. The belt is the M1845/48, with bayonet and *sabre-glaive* on the left and the cartridge box behind.

F2: *Fusilier, 1er Régiment Étranger*; barracks dress, Sathonay, early 1856

The new regiment's uniform was confirmed by regulations of 16 April 1856. This veteran serving as an officer's orderly wears an M1852 *képi* with a garance top and regimental number and a green band and piping. The fusiliers' *veste* was all-green, though elite companies wore red collar patches with green badges; it here displays two re-enlistment chevrons. The trousers of the rank-and-file were generously cut, but not of the officers' *mi-bouffant* shape. The Swiss unit's first *capote* was the M1845/52 in blued-iron grey with red collar patches; shortly before the 1859 Italian campaign they received the M1845/58 with green patches.

F3: *Lieutenant-colonel, 1er Régiment Étranger*; Sidi bel Abbès, late 1856

This regimental second-in-command in *grande tenue* shows the rear of the M1845/55 tunic, and the M1852 officers' *képi*; compare with frontal details on figure C3, and note that this officer too would have gold embroidered grenades set slanting on his collar. He also has alternating gold and silver *galons* on the cap, and the epaulettes have silver straps but gold crescents and short, thick fringes. He carries the straight-bladed M1855 senior officers' sabre, with a more ornate gilded hilt. Only field officers were normally mounted; the 'English' saddle is tan brown, the bridle and harness black with brass fittings. The green valise has a gold border and numeral and red piping. The saddle-cloth is green, with a gold regimental numeral in the angle of (for this rank) one 15mm silver and one 35mm gold border, with red outer piping. The colonel had both borders in gold, majors and *chefs de bataillon* a single 35mm gold border. The field saddle-cloths of officers of the 2e RE (1856–61) were black with garance borders and numeral, and without numbers thereafter.

Rear details of the yellow-collared M1860 *habit* (the so-called '*basquine*') with red Legion piping and fusilier turnback badges – see Plate G1. This jacket was part of a baroque uniform which was based on pure fashion rather than on practicality, and which only lasted for seven years. Army orders stated that this garment should replace the *veste* even for field use, but the troops normally based in North Africa were exempted from this regulation. (Drawing by Gerry Embleton)

F4: *Caporal, Compagnies de Chasseurs, 1er Régiment Étranger*; Kabylia, 1857

Engaged in the same campaign as figure D3, this is a soldier of the regiment's 594-strong *bataillon d'elite* led by Cdt Lion in 2nd Bde (Col Nesmes-Desmarets), 4th Div (Gen Maissiat) during Gen Randon's offensive. One source states that the 1er RE sent back to store both their shakos and their tunics before sailing for Africa that July, but Guyader (2005) shows this uniform. The Tirailleurs had been equipped like Chasseurs à Pied: an all-green *képi* except for yellow piping; an all-green tunic piped in yellow, with a cutaway collar, pointed cuffs and silver buttons; an unpiped green *veste*; and blue-grey trousers with yellow seam-piping. Rank stripes were also yellow (or for senior NCOs, gold backed with yellow), shaped *en pique* following the cuff shape. This man's pack stowage would include the Chasseurs' special dark blue-grey *capuchon*, an elbow-length sleeveless cape with a hood. Note the one-piece cotton *képi* cover and neck curtain, common by this date in both Foreign Regiments in Algeria; the Chasseurs' special open-frame belt buckle; and their shortened weapon, the M1853 T percussion carbine, with a brass-hilted 'yataghan' bayonet in a steel scabbard. When in the field the *giberne* was sometimes brought round to the right front of the belt, though its size would presumably prevent this when the *contre-sanglons* were worn.

G: *RÉGIMENT ÉTRANGER*, MEXICO, 1863–67
G1: *Caporal, Fusiliers*; Veracruz, March 1863

Napoleon III's decree of 30 March 1860 gave the rank-and-file of the whole French Line uniforms based on those of the Chasseurs à Pied de la Garde Impériale, who had won popular renown in Italy. The M1860 *habit*, later popularly known as the '*basquine*', was ordered worn by all rankers in the field in place of the *veste*. The worst atrocities were the very bouffant calf-length Chasseur-style trousers, which had to be worn with laced leather *jambières* over the top of the gaiters; this arrangement proved disastrously uncomfortable in Mexico, where the leggings were often discarded and men marched with their trousers loose at the calf.

This homage to Benigni shows a Legion veteran of the Italian campaign as he disembarks; note the Italy Medal, and the re-enlistment chevrons, now worn on the *habit* but not the *veste*. He is identified as a fusilier by his M1852 epaulettes, and by the absence of red elite-company badges from his collar. The Legion's tunics were piped in garance instead of the yellow used by the Line (see accompanying line drawing). Other peculiarities are his traditional *cartouchière*, and his headgear – a French Navy straw, often worn with a fitted white cloth cover. (The M1860 shako, regulation field wear for the Line, was obviously inconvenient in Mexico; some units purchased palm-leaf panama hats during stop-overs in the French West Indies en route, and local straw sombreros were widely acquired after arrival.) The *musette* haversack became regulation issue in 1861. The weapon is the M1842 T percussion rifle-musket.

G2: *Fusilier*, Camerone, April 1863

For service in the pestilential 'Hot Lands' between the coast and the Orizaba plateau the RE retained its Algerian field uniforms. Troops based in Africa were exempted from orders of 24 May and 3 November 1860 discontinuing use of the white fatigue trousers and the *veste*, and one of 18 October specifically allowed them to keep the *képi*. This tentative reconstruction represents a légionnaire at Camerone on 30 April, as described by the survivor Cpl Maine, though he inexplicably identified the 3rd Company's weapon as the Chasseur carbine rather than the standard rifle-musket. We have chosen to show the latter, and also (speculatively) replacement gaiters made up from old *capote*-cloth, as often seen. The green body-belt is a reminder that such sashes were still unregulated, and thus varied. Note the red collar patches worn on the *veste*, although the greatcoat had these *écussons* in midnight-blue.

G3 & G4: *Légionnaire* and *Caporal*, *6e Compagnie/2e Bataillon*, 1866

The common daily wear of the mounted squadron formed within the 2e Bn in May 1864 was as the painting by Benigni (see page 34), though sometimes with a local sombrero. White sabre and pouch belts came from Chasseurs d'Afrique stores, with M1855 sabres with three-bar brass hilts and steel scabbards. The Legion Museum's famous painting by Von Prost of a senior NCO in a dolman-style tunic had been dated to 1865, but Guyader (2005) suggests that it was not until the formation of a second squadron in summer 1866 – when an all-arms Legion brigade was being prepared for long-term Mexican service – that these well-attested cavalry modifications took place. The *képi* band was decorated with Hungarian knots in red lace. The tunic was transformed into a *dolman à brandenbourgs* by the addition of 17 lines of thin black cord frogging uniting three rows of brass half-ball buttons down the front, and black trefoils on the shoulder secured by two buttons. A red grenade also appeared on the collar and the tail turnbacks, and the cuff flaps became solid garance. This dolman was worn open below the first button, over a sash and the Chasseur sabre belt; the belts were now blackened, with a grenade badge on the pouch belt and pouch flap, and brass side-plates on the pouch. Despite these nods to hussar style, the character of the Legion squadrons was always that of dragoons, and they carried the infantry rifle-musket slung across their backs.

H: RÉGIMENT DE MARCHE ÉTRANGER, FRANCE, 1870–71

H1: Sergent-major, Army of the Loire; Coulmiers, November 1870

The impractical M1860 infantry uniform was replaced under various regulations issued between 31 May and 2 December 1867. The Legion's *képi* received a garance star badge; chinstraps were still non-regulation, but sometimes seen. The austere new M1867 regulation double-breasted tunic hardly differed for officers and senior NCOs except in quality; of midnight-blue with minimal garance piping, and two rows of seven brass buttons (not converging dramatically), it was specified for the Legion with garance collars piped blue. In July 1870 Army sergeant-majors were ordered to wear tunics in the field even when their men were in greatcoats. The nine-button *veste* of junior rankers (officially reintroduced on 17 June 1868) now lacked epaulette loops or collar patches; epaulettes were worn only on greatcoats and NCOs' tunics. On 30 January 1868 elite companies were discontinued throughout the Army, and thereafter all Legion rankers wore a new epaulette with a green strap and scarlet crescent and fringe. This decorated veteran of Mexico has dumped his pack, but retains his M1861 single-spout canteen (note also M1865 issue mug) and M1861 haversack. The rapid rate of fire of the new bolt-action M1866 Chassepot rifle prompted the addition of an M1867 oiled cloth 'cartridge pocket' to the right front of the belt to supplement the contents of the rear *giberne*.

H2: Soldat de 1ere classe, 5e Bataillon, Army of the East; Héricourt, January 1871

This new Army rank was introduced at the same time as the disappearance of elite companies in 1868, being identified by one red sleeve stripe. The appearance of the rebuilt Régiment de Marche Étranger in December–January was probably extremely motley, since its heavy casualties were replaced with drafts from the 7e, 12e, 21er, 68e, 69e and 71er Régts du Ligne and with raw conscripts. The M1867 *capote*, still in 'blued-iron grey', had a 45mm rounded stand collar with midnight-blue patches, and two rows of six brass buttons. Sheepskin jerkins were widely issued to French troops during that harsh winter, worn with a variety of greatcoats and trousers; according to the *Livre d'Or*, these included clothing from Garde Nationale Mobile stores (see MAA 237). Men kept themselves warm as best they could; this soldier in the hills above Belfort has acquired a scarf in a local 'windowpane' weave. The more experienced men were shared out among companies of the three battalions; survivors of the V/RE formed in France were distinguishable by silver buttons, a white '5' on the *képi*, and old M1852 fusiliers' epaulettes. One source mentions leather gaiters, presumably the old M1839 reintroduced in 1865; these had been standard infantry issue (alongside the white cloth gaiters) for bad weather and fatigues, but seem not to be illustrated in use by the Legion. We show the big February 1869 pattern leather 'cartridge pocket' on the

Watercolour by Titeux illustrating a corporal of Legion fusiliers, wearing the more practical replacement uniform of 1867 regulations – compare with Plate H1. However, he once again shows the regulation infantry shako of that date, which was not issued to the Legion. Neither was the M1867 tunic worn by légionnaires below the rank of sergeant, who instead paraded in the *capote* and wore either that or the *veste* when in the field. (Anne S.K. Brown Collection, Providence RI; photo René Chartrand)

front of the belt, again in addition to the *giberne* on the back.

H3: Capitaine, Army of Versailles; Paris, April–May 1871

This officer is not an Algeria veteran, but one of the many drafted in from various sources to rebuild the regiment in April. His tunic is as H1 above, but after the proclamation of the Third Republic in September 1870 many officers discarded their epaulettes and replaced them with cuff-rings of rank. He wears the M1845 *ceinturon de petite tenue* with its embossed gilt plate, but has left his sabre in his quarters. Instead he carries more practical private-purchase items: cased binoculars, and the holster for a big M858 12mm Lefaucheux pinfire revolver.

INDEX